TAVERNS *and* STAGECOACHES

of New England

7493/2

Ex Libris

Taverns and Stagecoaches

of

New England

ANECDOTES AND TALES

recalling the days of
Stagecoach Travel and the Ancient Hostelries
where Strangers Tarried

"Oh, the days are gone when the merry horn
Awakened the echoes of smiling morn,
As, breaking the slumber of village street,
The foaming leaders' galloping feet
Told of the rattling, swift approach
Of the well-appointed old stage-coach."

By
ALLAN FORBES
Edited by R. M. EASTMAN

Printed for the
STATE STREET TRUST COMPANY
BOSTON
1953

Copyright 1953

by the

STATE STREET TRUST COMPANY

Boston

Printed by
THE RAND PRESS
Boston

FOREWORD

THE DAYS of the stagecoach have faded far enough into the
past to gather a halo of history and romance, though some of
the passengers of this useful, though generally uncomfortable,
vehicle might not agree with the glorification of what they
considered an instrument of torture after a long and bumpy,
dusty or muddy, ride.

Forever associated with the stagecoach are the ancient
hostelries where passengers were wont to stop for rest and
refreshments, or for lodging overnight. Looking back with
romance-tinted glasses, we are prone to see cheery landlords
ready to greet us; food wholesome and tasty, if not fancy; beds
soft and comfortable after the day's ride. It is not likely to occur
to us that possibly some of the inns were untidy, the food dis-
appointing and the beds hard, with landlords sharp and grasping.

In any event, the stagecoach did provide a new and faster
mode of travel and the taverns were undoubtedly welcome
havens for the tired traveler. It is much more satisfactory to
recall the pleasant side of this era than to dwell on its disad-
vantages. With that in mind, we felt that a brochure on stagecoach and tavern days might be a fitting addition to the 36
previously issued on subjects such as Indian events, whaling,
clipper ships, merchants and sea captains, ship sailing an-
nouncements, early industries, etc., which have seemed to meet
with the favor of our readers and all of which are now collectors'
items. We hope you will enjoy our latest endeavor to provide
an interesting and entertaining publication.

The sources of material for brochures along historical lines,
such as we have been presenting for many years, are, of course,
the books, magazine articles, pamphlets, diaries and practically
all forms of publications, private or public, issued in years gone
by. It will be noted that throughout this brochure we have

mentioned various authors whose material has been consulted, and it is done not only to give credit to those whose research has been helpful to us but also in the hope that the excerpts used may lead our readers to seek out the works of the authors for their further interest and enjoyment. We feel sure that anyone doing so will get much satisfaction from the slight effort involved, since many of the publications mentioned are available in the public libraries with which our Commonwealth is so well supplied.

Inasmuch as a second volume on this subject is in the planning stage, should any of our readers have information, anecdotes or interesting incidents about stagecoaches or taverns in New England, not mentioned in this volume, it would be a favor if they would call our attention to them.

Acknowledgments

Again, special mention should be made of the cooperation given by James L. Bruce of the Bostonian Society; by members of the staff of the Boston Public Library and by Dennis A. Dooley, State Librarian and his associates. Also, we desire to give public recognition to the following members of our staff: Miss Alice G. Higgins for her assistance in research, Miss Katherine G. Rogers, Miss Dorothy Cilley, Miss Barbara M. Oberlander, Miss Alita Gray and Miss Helen J. Williamsen for their work in typing the manuscript and the correspondence necessary in the compilation of this brochure.

We also wish to express our sincere appreciation to those listed below for their helpfulness to us in our search for material for use in this year's publication:

E. Florence Addison, Alan G. Agnew, Mrs. Walter Austin, Miss Millicent J. Ayton, Ernest J. Baker, Miss Dorothy C. Barck, J. C. Bingham, Guy N. Bjorge, Miss Barbara Bonner, Clarence S. Brigham,

Prof. Bancroft H. Brown, E. D. W. Chaplin, Buchanan Charles, Charles W. Cheney, Charles H. P. Copeland, Col. Paul H. Downing, Miss Betty Dumaine, Mrs. Alexander M. Earle, Frederic B. Eastman, Robert M. Edgar, Mrs. Walter Forbes, C. C. Garner, Mrs. Charles Dana Gibson, John W. Hamilton, Hiram Harlow, Robert H. Haynes, August S. Hirschbaum, Edgar C. Hirst, Miss Elizabeth R. Humphreys, Walter Humphreys, Elmer M. Hunt, Miss Helena Mills John, Herbert E. Kahler, Mrs. Carl F. Kaufmann, Katherine M. Kuechle, George A. Kyle, Mrs. Jean M. Lambertt, Bertram K. Little, Robert W. Lovett, Donald H. McLaughlin, John Foster Meck, George Melcher, Keyes E. Metcalf, Sir Owen Morshead, T. R. Navin, Neal O'Hara, Smith Hempstone Oliver, Miss Nell Perrigoue, Miss Lois E. Peterson, E. W. Pilling, J. Lee Potter, O. J. Salisbury, Mrs. E. Ray Shaw, Dr. Clifford K. Shipton, Miss Irene Simpson, Everett W. Smith, Miss Dorothea E. Spear, Mrs. Thomas W. Streeter, Mrs. James A. Sullivan, Frank A. Taylor, C. L. Tower, T. T. Townsend, Miss Ethel M. Turner, Hon. Mrs. Peter Vanneck, Bert Vickery, Robert W. Weltshe, Walter Muir Whitehill, Sir Evelyn Wrench, C.M.G., LL.D., Franklin Wyman, Jr., Paul F. Young.

*I*T has been our custom to issue from time to time publications designed
to prove enjoyable and of historical value to our friends. We trust
that this thirty-seventh brochure will succeed in fulfilling this desire.

We also hope that the impression received will be so favorable that
the reader will feel that our publications typify the institution which
issues them and that the high standard maintained in their form and
material is characteristic of the banking and trust service we render.

We shall be very happy if the pleasure derived from our brochures
induces our friends to think favorably of the State Street Trust Company when the occasion arises for opening a new bank account, financing
the purchase of an automobile or household appliances, or renting a safe
deposit box at any of our four offices. We also have storage facilities for
silverware and other bulky valuables at our Main and Massachusetts
Avenue offices.

It may be that some of our readers are not aware of the fact that
our Trust Department is qualified by experience to serve effectively as
Agent in the handling of investments, as Trustee of Living Trusts,
Pension and Profit Sharing Plans, Life Insurance Trusts, as Executor
and Trustee under wills and in any other recognized trust capacity.

It will be a pleasure to us to furnish to those interested detailed
information in regard to any of the various services which we render.

ALLAN FORBES,
Chairman of the Board
State Street Trust Company

Boston, 1953

Taverns and Stagecoaches

of

New England

TABLE OF CONTENTS

LIST OF ILLUSTRATIONS

PAINTED IN 1826 BY WILLIAM BROWN OF CHARLESTOWN IN HIS 18TH YEAR.
From the collection of The Bostonian Society, Old State House, Boston

Taverns and Stagecoaches
of
New England

The PLEASANT and the UNPLEASANT SIDE of the STAGECOACH

MANY OF the things we do have their unpleasant as well as their pleasant sides and so it was with the lumbering stage wagons, which were called by many names, from violoncello cases, diving bells, and distillers' vats, to a ship beating against a heavy sea. An appropriate tale is told by Alice Morse Earle in her book about stagecoaches:

A New Englander asked the best way to a certain inn and was informed that he could proceed by "either sloop or barge" and that the barge was the quickest way. He figured out that the barge would be propelled by power, and was conducted into a stage coach which he expected would lead him to a wharf, from which he would change to a water trip. After going some distance, the traveller inquired of the driver how soon they would reach the wharf. The following conversation is copied from the above-mentioned book.

"When do we reach the wharf?"
"We ain't goin' to the wharf," he drawled.
"Where do we take the barge then, and when?"
"You're a-ridin' in the barge now," he answered.

When the weather was disagreeable, when the driver or the tavern keeper was in a bad mood, when the "flying machines," as they were sometimes called, were uncomfortable, and the horses were behaving badly, a journey in this contrivance could not have been much pleasure. In fact occasionally one heard the remark, "Is this a coach or a hollowedout iceberg?" However, when the travel conditions were good, the weather clear and warm, the driver and one's companions agreeable, and the coach rattling along on a good road and on time, a journey must have been a good deal of fun.

The most noted writer who describes a stagecoach journey in this country was Dickens who, in his *American Notes*, gives this account of a stagecoach trip in Virginia.

The passengers are getting out of the steamboat, and into the coaches; the luggage is being transferred in noisy wheelbarrows; the horses are frightened, and impatient to start; the black drivers are chattering to them like so many monkeys; and the white ones whooping like so many drovers; for the main thing to be done in all kinds of hostelering here, is to make as much noise as possible . . . They are covered with mud from the roof to the wheel-tire, and have never been cleaned since they were first built . . . I throw my coat on the box, and hoist my wife and her maid into the inside. It has only one step, and that being about a yard from the ground, is usually approached by a chair: when there is no chair, ladies trust in Providence.

They run up the bank, and go down again on the other side at a fearful pace. It is impossible to stop them, and at the bottom there is a deep hollow, full of water. The coach rolls frightfully. The insides scream. The mud and water fly about us. The black driver dances like a madman. Suddenly we are all right by some extraordinary means, and stop to breathe.

Continuing his journey westerly he refers again to his experiences:

As to doing the honours of his coach, his [the driver's] business, as I have said, is with the horses. The coach follows because it is attached to them on wheels: not because you are in it. Sometimes, towards the end of a long stage, he suddenly breaks out into a discordant fragment of an election song, but his face never sings along with him: it is only his voice, and not often that.

He always chews and always spits, and never encumbers himself with a pocket-handkerchief. The consequences to the box passenger, especially when the wind blows towards him, are not agreeable.

The well known English author, Thomas de Quincey, who spoke glowingly of his country's stagecoaches in *Modern Modes of Travelling*, wrote:

Modern modes of travelling cannot compare with the old mail-coach system in grandeur and power. They boast of more velocity, not, however, as a consciousness, but as a fact of our lifeless knowledge, resting upon *alien* evidence; as for instance, because somebody *says* that we have gone fifty miles in the hour, though we are far from feeling it as a personal experience; or upon the evidence of a result, as that we actually find ourselves in York four hours after leaving London. But seated on the old mail-coach we needed no evidence out of ourselves to indicate the velocity . . . and this speed was not the product of blind insensate energies that had no sympathy to give, but was incarnated in the fiery eyeballs of the noblest among brutes, in his dilated nostril, his spasmodic muscles and thunder-beating hoofs.

Another voyager from across the water is quoted by Frederick A. Currier in his talk before the Fitchburg Historical Society as describing his travels by stage over the present route of the Boston & Albany Railroad. "These Yankees talk," he said, "of constructing a railroad over this route; as a practical engineer, I pronounce it simply impossible." Yet the impossible did happen a short time later. Another doubting Thomas wrote an article in the *Boston Courier* in 1827, on the same subject.

Alcibiades, or some other great man of antiquity, it is said, cut off his dog's tail that the *quidnuncs* might not become extinct from want of excitement. Some such notion, no doubt, moved one or two of our national and experimental philosophers to get up the project of a railroad from Boston to Albany, a project which every one knows, who knows the simplest rule of arithmetic, to be impracticable, but at an expense little less than the market value of the whole territory of Massachusetts; and which, if practicable, every person of common sense knows would be as useless as a railroad from Boston to the moon.

A speaker of the time stated that the opening of such communication with Boston would affect the price of oats . . . The records of Quincy are said to contain, in black and white, the protest of a much worked-up citizen against allowing the Old Colony railroad to pass through the town, on the ground that the noise would prevent his hens from laying.

At least one English traveler was evidently quite satisfied with the stagecoach for he remarked that, "Seven and one-half miles per hour from Boston to Providence, I record as being considerably the quickest rate of travelling met with anywhere in America."

Another stage passenger made the remark that: "By this unparalleled speed a merchant may go to New York and return in less than ten days, which is truly wonderful." An advertisement declared that "It is the most convenient and expeditious way of travelling that can be had in America."

Daniel Webster hired a seat in a country sleigh in 1804 in order, shortly after the turn of the century, to travel to New Hampshire as he could find no other conveyance going to his destination. He wrote later: "Stage coaches no more ran into the center of New Hampshire at this time than they ran to Baffin's Bay."

A century and more before, Madame Knight wrote the story of her horseback ride from Boston to New York and back. At this early date she encountered much that was disagreeable not only on her long ride, but at the hostelries where she stopped. The food offered at the taverns was apt to be trying; in one place the "cabbage was of so deep a purple," she thought it had been "boiled in the dye-kettle." She speaks of a "cannoo" so small and shallow that she kept her "eyes stedy, not daring so much as to lodg my tongue a hair's breadth more on one side of my mouth than tother, nor so much as think of Lott's wife, for a wry thought would have oversett our wherey." When she again reached home, she wrote these lines:

> Now I've returned to Sarah Knight's
> Thro' many toils and many frights;
> Over great rocks and many stones,
> God has presarv'd from fractured bones.

Another verse from Mrs. Knight was inspired by a row that she witnessed on her way home:

> I ask thy Aid, O Potent Rum;
> To charm these wrangling Topers Dum.
> Thou hast their Giddy Brains possest —
> The man confounded with the Beast —
> And I, poor I, can get no rest.
> Intoxicate them with thy fumes,
> O still their Tongues till morning comes!"

W. Outram Tristram deplored the passing of the stage, of which he so thoroughly approved.

"Them," he cries, with a fine directness of pathos, "them as 'ave seen coaches afore rails came into fashion 'ave seen something worth remembering! Them was 'appy days for old England afore reform and rails turned everything upside down, and men road as nature intended they should, on pikes, with coaches and smart active cattle, and not by machinery like bags of cotton and hardware. But coaches is done for ever, and a heavy blow it is! They was the pride of the country; there wasn't anything like them, as I've 'eerd gemmen say from forrin parts, to be found nowhere, nor never will again."

One author compares a fast coach to a clipper ship off to China, but the skipper of both conveyances "wants to be sure of his rigging first." The coaches that had acquired the greatest reputation for speed were often called MERCURY, QUICKSILVER or COMET, etc.

Almost every traveler complained of the early starts. An Englishman speaks of leaving Boston for New York at the unearthly hour of two a.m. and a dismal picture is presented by Alice Morse Earle entitled, *A Wet Start at Daybreak*. A few accounts of early starts are very descriptive. Longfellow wrote of his drive to the Wayside Inn:

The Stage left Boston about three o'clock in the morning, reaching the Sudbury Tavern for breakfast, a considerable portion of the route being travelled in total darkness, and without your having the least idea who your companion might be.

Several accounts relate that the passenger on the top of the coach was not aware until dawn approached that there were two leaders of a six-in-hand. There were many complaints when a lodger was waked up to find it necessary to move over to make room for a second occupant of the bed.

Of course many were the accidents and difficulties encountered. Storms and floods were serious, but forest fires, we are told, were the most frightening. One hears that sometimes the occupants chose to sit with their backs to the horses so as not to be able to see the dangers ahead. Another traveler related his sufferings:

> We travelled all night. The rain and snow descending through the roof, our hats were frozen to our capes, and our cloaks to one another. In the morning we looked like some mountain of ice moving down the Gulf Stream. I thought the machine used at the Dry Dock would have been an excellent appendage to have lifted us bodily into the breakfast room: and this is what the horse-flesh fraternity in New York advertise as their *safe, cheap, comfortable* and expeditious winter establishment for Albany.

Racing was so serious at one time that a stage line advertised that *no racing* was allowed. In spite of everything it must have been very jolty at times causing a writer to remark that one of the passengers ate too heavily and consequently his "stomach was in fine agitation for the remaining fifty miles." "Springing 'em" was the usual expression for speeding up.

POETRY OF THE ROAD

EVERY ERA brings forth verses, some humorous, some sarcastic, and in this chapter a number of lines have been collected from the accounts of stagecoach travel handed down by others. The stage driver, the innkeeper, the traveler, the refreshments have not been overlooked in these stanzas which have been grouped together in the belief that this would be the most interesting method of presentation.

The best known verses about the old methods of travel were, of course, written by Oliver Wendell Holmes in his *One Horse Shay*, and we are venturing to quote them:

> Now in building of chaises, I tell you what,
> There is always somewhere a weakest spot, —
> In hub, tire, felloe, in spring, or thill,
> In panel, or cross-bar, or floor, or sill,
> In screw, bolt, thoroughbrace — lurking still.
> Find it somewhere you must and will, —
> Above or below, or within or without —
> And that's the reason, beyond a doubt,
> A chaise breaks down, but doesn't wear out.

In a chapter entitled, *The Puritan Ordinary*, Alice Morse Earle quotes a poet as expressing his views of life at an inn —

> Our life is nothing but a winter's day,
> Some only break their fast and so away;
> Others stay dinner and depart full fed;
> The deepest age but sups and goes to bed.
> He's most in debt who lingers out the day,
> Who dies betimes, has less and less to pay.

Another more complimentary verse about the inn and the innkeeper is credited to William Shenstone, the English poet:

> Whoe'er has travell'd life's dull round,
> Where'er his stages may have been,
> May sigh to think he still has found
> The warmest welcome at an inn.

The most humorous words had much to say about the concoctions mixed by the innkeeper, and the "Bee Hive" Tavern in Philadelphia had an amusing sign reading:

> Here in this hive we're all alive,
> Good liquor makes us funny.
> If you are dry, stop in and try
> The flavor of our honey.

The beehive decoration was used also at Charlestown, N. H. and this signboard is now in the Worcester Historical Society, Worcester, Mass. A similar emblem was used by the ship merchants, Sutton & Co., on the announcement cards of their clipper ship sailings.

Another verse was recited by a tippler at a bar a long distance from Boston, to the surprise of his fellow tipplers:

> Our fathers of old, they lived like goats.
> They washed their eyes and then their throats.
> But we, their sons, have grown more wise,
> We wash our throats and then our eyes.

A glass of wine as a traveler departed from an inn caused him to remark:

> If well apply'd, makes their dull horses feel
> One spur i'th Head is worth two in the heel.

An amusing toast frequently heard in taverns ran as follows: "To the enemies of our country: May they have cobweb breeches, porcupine saddles, hard trotting horses and an eternal journey." Its first use is attributed to Captain William Watson who is said to have given it during the Revolution at a banquet in the Eagle Tavern at East Poultney, Vermont.

This following ancient rhyme (part of a longer one) quoted by Edward Field was repeated in *Among Old New England Taverns* by Mary Caroline Crawford, published by L. C. Page & Co. in 1907:

> Landlord, to thy bar room skip,
> Make it a foaming mug of flip —

Make it of our country's staple,
Rum, New England sugar maple,
Beer that's brewed from hops and Pumpkins,
Grateful to the thirsty Bumpkins.
Hark! I hear the poker sizzle
And O'er the mug the liquor drizzle,
And against the earthen mug
I hear the wooden spoon's cheerful dub.
I see thee, landlord, taste the flip;
And fling thy cud from under lip,
Then pour more rum, the bottle stopping,
Stir it again and say it's topping;
Come, quickly bring the humming liquor,
Richer than ale of British vicar, . . .

ANECDOTES OF THE ROAD

NEW ENGLAND LANDLORDS had a fine sense of humor, but of course the traveler had to bear the brunt of the pranks. An exceedingly stout individual once entered an inn on Tremont Street, Boston, and, as the story goes, inquired the price of a meal. To his surprise a tape measure was brought up with which to measure the circumference of his waist. After consulting the figures on the tape, it was decided that the charge to a man of his proportion would be four dollars. Another very large gentleman, bent on having as comfortable a journey as possible, believed he had better secure two seats for his long ride. He was sold two, but to his disgust when he reached the coach, he discovered that a joke had been played on him and one seat was inside and the other was outside! At best traveling must have been pretty rough, for one weary customer was heard to remark that it was a "comfort to shift one's position and be bruised in a new place." Another traveler, this time from Vermont, started to leave an inn forgetting to pay for his breakfast. The proprietor, known familiarly as "Uncle Peter," thereupon remarked: "Mister, if you should lose your pocketbook between here and Greenfield, remember you didn't take it out here." From Boston came the story of a stout woman who at dawn unfortunately sat herself down on an egg, which the proprietor's hen had laid in the seat the evening before. Doubtless many informalities were met with. There is a story of a woman who at breakfast accidentally dropped an egg on the floor in her endeavor to take it from its shell. "What shall I do?" she exclaimed. The man sitting next to her promptly exclaimed, "Cackle!"

A trick occasionally played on the innocent passenger was to call out "Stage ready" before the traveler had quite finished his meal, being sure, however, that it had been paid for. Some announcer to speed the guest would sometimes add, "Liquor tossed down quickly works double inside!" Stephen Jenkins in *The Old Boston Post Road* tells of a bridge near the East River in New York known to most travelers as the "Kissing Bridge," because, when going over it in the coach, it was a regular custom to bestow a kiss upon your nearest lady companion, which a traveler remarked was "curious but not displeasing."

Passengers had to take what was coming in the way of bad roads and stormy weather. A stage sometimes got stuck in the mud and on one occasion the driver asked his passengers to alight and help extricate the vehicle, which they refused to do. The driver, thereupon, got out and sat by the roadside, calmly smoking. Words followed in quick succession, whereupon the driver remarked: "Since them horses can't pull that 'kerrige out o' that mud-hole, an' ye won't help, I'm a-goin' to wait till th' mud-hole dries up."

Competition later made the drivers very accommodating and they really acted as expressmen for their customers. Naturally mistakes were bound to be made in the desire to make all speed possible. There is a well-known story that mentions an occurrence at a country post office. The postmistress, being awakened late at night, by mistake threw out, instead of the mail bag, her laundry bag which when opened furnished quite a surprise. At another time a baby was delivered to the wrong house, then occupied by an old bachelor. A guest at an inn related how another guest won a wager that a certain bottle would hold a quart and this is the way he won his bet. After filling the bottle he put the cork in, turned it upside down and filled the hollow space in the bottom with the rest of the quart, thereby winning his wager.

Many surprises took place on the road when stages encountered droves of cattle and sheep and on one occasion a stagecoach ran into a curious caravan on a covered bridge when an elephant hit his head on one of the roof beams and lying down seemed to take pleasure in thereby delaying the stage.

The Concord stagecoach, product of Yankee ingenuity and craftsmanship, helped mightily in the "Winning of the West." For ten years, until the country was spanned by steel rails in 1869, hundreds of these coaches shuttled back and forth between St. Joe, Mo. and Sacramento — 1900 miles in about 16 days.

This particular coach ran between Hangtown, California (now Placerville) and Carson City, Nevada, carrying 16 passengers inside and on top. In addition, in the front and rear "boots" were luggage, mail bags—and the Wells Fargo treasure boxes, guarded by the shotgun messenger, who sat alongside the driver.

OLD HANGTOWN WELLS FARGO OVERLAND STAGE

Courtesy of Elmer Munson Hunt

THE CONCORD (NEW HAMPSHIRE) STAGECOACHES

CONCORD BUGGIES, Concord wagons and then Concord coaches caused their makers, Lewis Downing, his son, and J. Stephen Abbot to become well known in many parts of the world. Through the kindness of Elmer Munson Hunt, Director of the New Hampshire Historical Society, we have had the unusual opportunity of reading an early record book of Abbot-Downing Company recording sales, prices and purchases, now in the collection of the Historical Society.

An early entry, underlined in red to signify its importance, tells of the sale of the first Concord wagon on November 8, 1813 for sixty dollars to Benjamin Kimball, Jr., a relative of President Lewis Downing. As Mr. Hunt expressed it in his address before the Newcomen Society in 1945, the presiding genius "established one of the great pioneer industries of America" and "out of his labor and skill were wrought the direct ancestors of the railway carriages, motor cars and aircraft of our time."

Whoever kept this record book was accurate as to details of sales, except that his spelling was original, to say the least. For instance, one notices the words *exetrees, shaise* (for chaise), *harnes, whiffletrees, ballance, boddyes* and *wride;* the word "sales" is sometimes spelled "sails." One account was finally "ballanced by death." Among the customers appear many nationally known names of people living in the days from the Civil War to the 1890's.

The first Abbot-Downing stagecoach was built during the winter of 1826-1827 and in July of the latter year it was ready to deliver to John Shepherd of Salisbury, New Hampshire, who was reported as having "a fancy for stage business." He also kept an inn there, but his chief reputation seems to have been based upon the sole fact that once he was the owner of this first stagecoach ever to be built in New Hampshire. As Mr. Hunt further points out, in design and otherwise Mr. Downing followed the English vehicles of the type mentioned by Dickens in his "Pickwick Papers" as "rattling about." Improvements were introduced by the Company's President until the Abbot-Downing coach "was a better thing than the world had ever known — better to ride in, better to look at, better to hold the road under all conditions, and better to keep in repair."

Downing made the woodwork in his small but growing plant and as he had no means of manufacturing the iron parts, he ingeniously arranged with the inmates of the New Hampshire State Prison to do this special work, and when the two kinds of materials were placed in their proper positions in the structure of the coach, it has been said that the wood had been so carefully selected that it was almost as strong and lasting as the iron.

Orders for coaches came from many countries of the world, including Peru, Chile, New South Wales, England, Australia, Mexico, South Africa and other places.

Perhaps the most famous of the orders they filled was for the "Deadwood" coach which is described in our chapter entitled *Buffalo Bill and His Famous Deadwood Stagecoach.*

Next in importance are a few of the subsequent stages which are in existence today. Conspicuously placed and in fine condition in the Boston & Maine Railroad station in Concord, N. H. is a coach which originally carried the United States mail. It was built in 1852 and was presented to the Railroad by Harold Jefferson Coolidge of Boston, who had his summer place at Squam Lake in Sandwich, New Hampshire. It was accepted for the Railroad by Laurence F. Whittemore, then one of its executives, now President of the Brown Company of Berlin, New Hampshire. The vehicle, now over one hundred years old, was skillfully restored and is an attractive and appropriate reminder of the early means of locomotion over the New Hampshire roads and turnpikes. This information, as well as the picture reproduced here, was provided by one of the directors of the State

Street Trust Company, Everett W. Smith, Treasurer of the Boston & Maine Railroad.

A most recent public appearance of an Abbot-Downing stage coach occurred at the time Princess Elizabeth (now Queen) and the Duke of Edinburgh visited Canada in 1951. During their stay the Royal couple were conveyed in a century-old mail coach, formerly used on the run between Halifax, Truro and Pictou, Nova Scotia. There are several pictures of this celebrated vehicle showing the visiting Royalty in Calgary, Alberta. Only once before did the coach have a similar honor paid it when the present Queen's great-grandfather, the late King Edward VII, then Prince of Wales, rode in it from Truro to Pictou on his visit to Nova Scotia in 1860. This ancient relic is now owned by E. E. Gammon, proprietor of the Homestead Hotel in Banff. A newspaper article from *The Calgary Herald* contained the account of this 1951 visit:

> One of the best known connections with the historic past of Pictou County in Nova Scotia, the famous old Concord stage-coach in which the late King Edward VII, when Prince of Wales, made the journey from Truro to Pictou Aug. 6, 1860, will carry the great-granddaughter of its first royal passenger and her husband.
>
> For Princess Elizabeth and the Duke of Edinburgh are scheduled to ride in that coach and four when they arrive in Calgary during their tour of Canada. Immediately following the chuck-wagon dinner in the Stampede Corral, the royal couple will be whisked into the rose plush recesses of the coach and wheeled into the infield in front of the grandstand, from which vantage point they will see a miniature stampede . . .
>
> The blue paint and gilt lettering on the sides of the coach are all present day trimmings, for its everyday garb in the days of the gay '50's and '60's, before railways were even thought of, was good old fashioned Nova Scotian mud.
>
> . . . there was never a passenger injured nor a letter lost during the 36 years the Halifax, Truro and Pictou mail coach was on the road.

Courtesy of E. E. Gammon, Proprietor The Homestead Hotel, Banff, Alberta, Canada.

CENTURY OLD HISTORIC CONCORD STAGECOACH WHICH TWICE CARRIED ROYALTY ON THEIR VISITS TO CANADA.

The late King Edward VII when Prince of Wales rode in it in 1860 on his visit to Nova Scotia. In 1951 Princess Elizabeth, now Queen, and her husband, the Duke of Edinburgh, were conveyed in this

At the time of the royal visit in 1860, the coach was withdrawn from service and redecorated for the Prince of Wales. It was re-painted in royal blue and gilded with the royal coat of arms. For the occasion, it was drawn by six black horses, each crowned with a white silk flag bearing the insignia of the royal guest.

. . . .

But the big attraction will be the Halifax, Truro and Pictou mail coach with its royal passengers, and no doubt many a former Nova Scotian in Calgary will be pleased and proud to see the old Concord coach still in service and still serving royalty to the best of its 100-year-old ability.

We have within recent months seen a letter from Fred W. Watson of Arkansas City which shows the interest still taken in a Concord coach:

While in El Paso, Texas for the holidays I noticed an old stage coach parked in about the middle of the Plaza, which was attract-ing more spectators than a new model auto, and naturally it appealed to me as it is in such very fine condition.

Looking over the coach I discovered it was made in Concord by Abbot-Downing Co. . . .

In fact the more I looked, the more interesting it seemed the history of the old coach became, it now belongs to "The Sheriff's Posse" or at least that is the name on the side of the coach, and it has been kept painted a beautiful maroon, trimmed in yellow curved lines.

The coach is to be used or displayed in the New Year's Parade . . . The Plaza where the coach was on display is right in the middle of down town El Paso . . .

Considerable publicity was given to the Concord coach which was the first one to achieve the ascent of Mt. Washington "tooled" by George W. Lane who was in charge of the six-in-hand. The rough road, of which there is a picture in existence, shows that the drive was a difficult one. The occasion was the opening day, August 8, 1861, of a building called "The Tip-Top House," frequented especially by week-end parties.

A newspaper clipping in the Abbot-Downing notebook under date of 1890 speaks of the Center Harbor coach which "has been in constant use for the past 41 years, and looks today as good as new. They propose to use it 41 years more, and with the same care it has had, it will doubtless pull through." The *Concord Evening Monitor* of July 21, 1900 contained this paragraph:

> The major says that he had a ride in the old coach, which he enjoyed very much, and thinks with a few general repairs it will stand the racket for many years to come, and welcome each day the guests to the Senter House, as they come and go on their journey to the White Mountains and northern New Hampshire. The major also thinks, with the fifty years old Concord buggy of 1899, the half century old Senter House coach of 1900, and the world renowned "Deadwood Coach," of Buffalo Bill, built in 1863, the Concord reputation for building the very best of work is complete and worthy of record.

It should be mentioned here that a number of hotels in New York such as the Brevoort House and the Astor House purchased stages from this New Hampshire company; also in Boston the United States Hotel, the Tremont House and the Vendome owned Concord stages, as well as hotels in many other parts of the country.

In his research on the Concord Coach Mr. Hunt points out that on many occasions when a new coach arrived at its destination, the whole town headed by a brass band turned out to welcome the new arrival. Well it might be, for there were many variations in ornamentations. The doors furnished excellent backgrounds for decorations. Some purchasers desired bright colored flowers or landscapes to be placed there. "Ornament up rich and tasty" writes one customer. Another buyer required that on the footboard be painted a dancer on horseback; another preferred a picture of Phil Sheridan. Potter Palmer of the Palmer House in Chicago purchased four coaches to be of canary yellow and on each door was to be a painting of the hotel done "in John Burgum's best manner." (Mr. Burgum was then the foreman decorator for Abbot-Downing). The Windsor Hotel in New York wished paintings of horses on one door and dogs on the other. These specifications are taken from Mr.

Hunt's address previously referred to. It is agreed that the Concord coaches played an important part in uniting the east and west, and many bullet holes attest to the dangers they encountered.

The residents of Concord and nearby towns were treated to an unusual sight on April 15, 1868, when thirty beautiful stagecoaches made by Abbot-Downing left Concord on fifteen platform cars, with sixty harnesses, and spare parts valued at about $45,000. consigned to Wells Fargo & Co. at Omaha and Salt Lake City. This was said to have been the largest order for coaches ever sent out by one manufacturer at one time.

Elmer Munson Hunt mentions the decorations at the time of this unusual shipment to Wells Fargo & Co. —

The coaches are finished in a superior manner, the bodies red, and the running part yellow. Each door has a handsome picture, mostly landscapes, and no two of the thirty are alike. They are gems of beauty, and would afford study for hours; they were painted by Mr. J. Burgum.

The scroll work, executed by Mr. Chas. Knowlton, is very handsome, and varied on each coach.

Each one bore the name of some place, such as "The Deadwood" etc.

Miss Irene Simpson of the History Room of the Wells Fargo Bank & Union Trust Co., established in 1852, has sent us a short story of the Concord coach which was printed in the company's *Messenger* in March of 1952:

Time was when Wells Fargo coaches rolled all over the West. And its string of horses was second only to the U. S. Cavalry. The men who drove them were a fearless, determined group. Men like Hank Monk and James Miller, who whipped through marauding Piutes and outlaws alike to deliver the goods. The punishment of hard driving over wild country demanded tough equipment. And the Concord Coach was tough through and through — from the seasoned white ash spokes to the ox-hide boot.

. . . The overland mail coach was painted an English vermilion with straw colored running gear . . .

The Concord Coach is one of the most vivid symbols of the old West . . . Time was when the Concord was an important part of Wells Fargo's affairs.

John Gilmer, a noted driver, is supposed to have "turned the first wheel" of a Wells Fargo Overland stage. Agnes Wright Spring, in her excellent story of coaches, speaks of another well-known driver "who can handle six horses to a Concord coach, equal to the best known in the Rocky Mountain Country," adding that his co-workers asserted that he had such an appetite that he could "eat a stage horse broiled on toast every morning for breakfast."

Wells Fargo & Co. so developed its banking business that it is now one of the finest private institutions of its kind on this continent. In its museum in San Francisco is exhibited among the interesting relics of the West, the stagecoach occasionally used by Buffalo Bill in his Wild West show, probably while the "Deadwood" coach was being repaired. Our informant in charge of the exhibit in that bank, sends some amusing suggestions for the Plains' Traveler taken from a *Black Hills Pioneer* item printed in the *Omaha Herald* for October 3, 1877:

The best seat inside a stage is the one next to the driver. Even if you have a tendency to seasickness when riding backwards — you'll get over it and will get less bumps and jostling. Don't let any "sly Elph" trade you his mid-seat.

In cold weather don't ride with tight fitting boots, shoes or gloves. When the driver asks you to get off and walk do so without grumbling. He won't request it unless absolutely necessary. If the team runs away — sit still and take your chances. If you jump, nine out of ten times you will get hurt.

In very cold weather abstain entirely from liquor when on the road; because you will freeze twice as quickly when under its influence.

Don't growl at the food received at the station; stage companies generally provide the best they can get. Don't keep the stage waiting. Don't smoke a strong pipe inside the coach — spit on the leeward side. If you have anything to drink in a bottle pass it around. Procure your stimulants before starting as "ranch" (stage depot) whiskey is not always "nectar."

Don't swear nor lop over neighbors when sleeping. Take small change to pay expenses. Never shoot on the road as the noise may frighten the horses. Don't discuss politics or religion. Don't point out where murders have been committed, especially if there are any women passengers. Don't lag at the wash basin. Don't grease your hair, because travel is dusty. Don't imagine for a moment that you are going on a picnic. Expect annoyance, discomfort and some hardship.

Edward Hungerford, formerly historian for the Wells Fargo Bank wrote a number of excellent articles concerning the Concord coach, of which a number of paragraphs are quoted:

In addition to owning the finest horses, the California Stage Company bought the finest Concord coaches. The first Concord coach had arrived in San Francisco in 1850. It came from Boston around the Horn. The coach took its name from the capital of New Hampshire where it was manufactured, and it made the name famous all over the Americas, in Europe and even in India.

It was the Concord coach which made staging possible over primitive roads and mountain trails. With only the European type of coach, staging in the West probably never would have succeeded. The Concord was built for trouble, close to the ground for sharp curves at high speed, with a light upper structure and heavy underparts, with a springing arrangement made of heavy leather straps called thoroughbraces to absorb the shocks of the rough roads. It was an American coach, designed to fill the specific needs of staging in the West.

... the final touch were oil paintings on the panels of the doors. One was always a distant view of Mount Washington and the others — can you guess? — that sturdy New England crag, the Old Man of the Mountain.

... Thirty-five passengers have been known to ride on just one coach. The capacity was elastic.

In his book entitled *From Covered Wagon to Streamliner* Mr. Hungerford wrote:

The old-time firm of Wells Fargo and Company was probably the largest single purchaser of Concord coaches. It had taken upon itself the widespread and difficult business of transporting gold for the miners from the hills of California to the assay offices in Sacramento and in San Francisco — afterwards it spread its

Courtesy of Everett W. Smith, Treasurer of the Boston & Maine Railroad and a Director of the State Street Trust Company

CONCORD COACH IN THE BOSTON & MAINE STATION IN CONCORD, NEW HAMPSHIRE, BUILT BY ABBOT-DOWNING COMPANY.

Presented by Harold Jefferson Coolidge of Boston and Sandwich, New Hampshire, "for exhibition purposes." It was accepted for the Railroad by Laurence F. Whittemore, then one of its executives, now President of the Brown Company of

business eastward until finally its lines reached the Missouri. The journey over plain and desert and mountain from St. Joseph, Missouri, to Sacramento, the capital of California, generally took somewhere between three to four weeks. . . . At one time, Wells Fargo had more than a thousand of these coaches in its service. . . . The chief destination of these coaches, once in service, was Sacramento. There, connection was made with the night boat for San Francisco. Sometimes a hundred coaches would reach the K Street wharf to meet the boat. The hoofbeats of four or five hundred horses made a mighty clatter in the town and sent up volumes of dust from its unpaved streets. Of one of these Wells Fargo coaches, making its way into a Montana mining camp, one writer said:

"If there is a prettier street picture of animation than a red Concord coach with six spirited horses in harness and a good reinsman on the box, we have not seen it. But it was not always clean Concords and six prancing horses. There are the jerkeys and mud wagons with two and four horses, and passengers packed in like sardines, or footing it through the mud at the rate of two miles an hour in the dark background of memory on which the bright picture is painted."

But Wells Fargo and Company did not run heavily to jerkeys nor to mud wagons. Its coaches were almost invariably Concord and were well maintained. They ran on schedule, almost with the precision of a railroad train. But their day was not to be a long one. When, in the middle of the sixties, the Union Pacific Railroad began its slow but sure advance across the plains, westward from the Missouri, the stagecoach receded before the railroad until it was finally no longer used in transcontinental service but was relegated to side lines and back country where it hung on for a few brief years before its final extinction.

The following interesting caption appeared underneath the picture *The Concord Coach Covered the Continent:*

Concomitant with six-shooters in the history of the Early West were the Concord stagecoaches. Used by the overland express of Wells Fargo and Company, forerunners of the Railway Express Agency, their cargo often offered temptation to the gangster of the day.

These sturdy Yankee-built vehicles originated in Concord, New Hampshire. They accommodated nine passengers on three inside seats, and another traveler on top with the driver. Equipped to traverse rough roads at high speed, they would sway precariously along narrow, curving highways at an average rate of eight to ten miles an hour. Fresh teams of six fast horses were supplied at relay stations spaced twelve miles apart along the main routes.

In describing the coach one writer explained that it weighed 2,500 pounds, sold for about $1,250., carried nine passengers inside and as many more outside as could "cling to the roof."

The New Hampshire Journal as far back as 1829 contains an excellent description of one of these coaches. It reads, "Our friend Walker" . . . "in his zeal to render all good and worthy citizens of this (New Hampshire) and other states, who wish to ride either for his advantage or their own, comfortable, has lately placed upon the above line (Newport and Concord) a new and elegant coach; we have examined it, ridden in it, and find it to be such a one as cannot fail to please all who may wish to be transported." The paragraph ends by hoping the drivers "will meet the encouragement which they richly and justly merit."

Miss Irene Simpson gives us a list of a few other coaches which she discovered in a book in their library called *The Cheyenne and Black Hills Stage and Express Routes* by Agnes Wright Spring, published by the Arthur H. Clark Company, Glendale, California:

> The following old coaches, used on the Cheyenne to Deadwood route, are still in existence. . . .
>
> SOUTH DAKOTA, DEADWOOD. An old coach often used in parades.
>
> WASHINGTON, TACOMA. Museum of the Washington State Historical Society.
>
> WYOMING, CODY. Old coach at the Cody museum.
>
> WYOMING, CHEYENNE. Coach enclosed in small cabin in grounds at Union Pacific depot.
>
> WYOMING, LUSK. Small log museum houses coach presented to Lusk Lions Club by Russell Thorp, Jr.
>
> WYOMING, ROCK RIVER. Old coach under a small shed on U. S. 30, at eastern entrance to town.
>
> WYOMING, YELLOWSTONE NATIONAL PARK. Coach No. 259 on the portico of the museum at Mammoth Hot Springs

The Smithsonian Institution has a Concord coach marked 1848 which was loaned to the Museum by Will Rogers and Fred Stone in 1930. In 1945 the loan was changed to a gift. Mr. Edwin G. Burgum, an ornamental painter, son of John Burgum the original coach painter with Abbot-Downing, examined this coach in 1935 and reported that it was the oldest one he had so far discovered, and he had looked for coaches and examined many in all parts of the country.

In our search for the original Deadwood coach we had a letter from Miss Millicent Jean Ayton, a cousin of Mrs. Jean Lambertt in the household of Mr. and Mrs. Tudor Leland, and were intrigued to notice the heading on her letter paper "Harvard, Nebraska." Upon inquiry as to the origin of the name we received this reply which we believe will be of interest to a number of people:

It is named for Harvard University. The story is that the Burlington Rail Road attempted to name their stations this side of Omaha alphabetically beginning with Ashland. So there were (and still are) Ashland, Burr, Crete, Dorchester, Exeter, Friend, Grafton and the newest station would, of course, be named something beginning with "H".

Among the engineers employed by the Burlington was a young man from Massachusetts, a graduate of Harvard University, and who was terribly homesick, so he suggested that the town be "named Harvard, for my old Alma Mater." Thus our little town is a namesake of Harvard University.

The name of the Harvard man unfortunately is unknown. Of further interest is another fact. During the war a name was being chosen for a paper to be issued at the Army Air Field in Harvard, Nebraska when a Philadelphia boy who chanced to hear the discussion laughingly remarked "I'd call it 'The Accent' because there is a common saying in the east that you can always tell a Harvard man by his accent." And so the paper got the name "The Harvard Accent."

A few paragraphs should be devoted to the men who started Abbot-Downing: Lewis Downing, originally from Lexington,

Obtained by Everett Dickinson through his friend Smith Hempstone Oliver, Associate Curator, Section of Land Transportation, Smithsonian Institution, U. S. National Museum, Washington, D. C.

CONCORD STAGECOACH IN SMITHSONIAN INSTITUTION, WASHINGTON, D. C.

(See opposite page for description & history)

Mass., went to Concord in 1813, with $60. and a few tools saved while working in his father's blacksmith shop and then at the same trade in Charlestown. An early ad read that he —

. . . respectfully informs the inhabitants of Concord and its vicinity that he has commenced the wheelwright business in Concord where he flatters himself that by strict and constant attention to business and the correct and faithful manner in which his work will be executed, to merit the patronage of the public.
N.B. Carriages of all kinds repaired on the shortest notice.

About the year 1825 he conceived the idea of making coaches, soon to be known as the "travelers conveyance delux" and to assist him in his purpose he engaged J. Stephen Abbot of Salem, a young man who had studied that trade there. John Burgum, an Englishman already mentioned, soon to become a valued decorator of stages, joined the enterprise which by this time was employing about a dozen men, who worked long hours and in the winters by oil lamps.

A partnership between Abbot and Downing was formed in 1828, coach building being the chief feature of the firm. In 1847 the partnership was dissolved whereupon Downing took his two sons, Lewis and Alonzo, into a new firm known as L. Downing & Sons, thereby causing considerable rivalry. In 1865 the elder Downing retired and his sons realizing the value of the Abbots (father and son) consolidated under the familiar

---

Probably the oldest Concord stagecoach still extant is this one in the Smithsonian Institution, Washington, D. C., said to have been built in 1848 — the body by J. S. & A. E. Abbot and the running gear by Lewis Downing and Sons. On the running gear appears the name of F. S. Gerald who was a blacksmith with both Lewis Downing & Sons and Abbot-Downing Company. The right door panel, under the upholstery, is marked with the name of John L. French and the date 1848. French was a body builder with J. S. & A. E. Abbot and also with Abbot-Downing Company.
This coach first came to the Smithsonian Institution as a loan from those famous actors, Will Rogers and Fred Stone. It was then in California and was shipped from San Francisco to New York on the Army transport "St. Mihiel" in July of 1930. It is believed to be the only stagecoach ever to make such a trip via Army transport. In 1945 the loan was changed to a gift. Unfortunately no past history of the coach was ever obtained from the donors.

name of Abbot-Downing & Co. The company also made all kinds of wagons, too numerous to mention, including ambulances, gun carriages, etc. for the Civil War, also circus wagons. The Company had an office at one time in New York and one in Boston at 388 Atlantic Avenue.

An interesting series of coincidences connects Wells Fargo with the Concord coach. Mr. Hunt discovered after his address before the Newcomen Society, already referred to, that upon the death of Lewis Downing the assets of Abbot-Downing reverted to Samuel C. Eastman, President of the Historical Society, who bequeathed them to that Society in his will. The Historical Society did not wish to operate the business and sold the assets to Josiah Fernald, President of one of the Concord, New Hampshire, banks. In 1945 Mr. Fernald then sold the name Abbot Downing for a nominal fee to Elmer R. Jones, President of the Wells Fargo Company, which company now retains it, as a matter of sentimental interest, serving as an important link between New England and the West.

STAGEMEN'S ENTERTAINMENTS

THE EAGLE COFFEE HOUSE, later to be known by the simpler name of Eagle Hotel, was built in 1827. Five years later the *New Hampshire Patriot* contains this amusing advertisement showing improvements and change of ownership.

Eagle

Coffee-House

kept by

A good portly man, i'faith and a pleasant; of a cheerful look, a pleasing eye, and a most noble carriage; and, as I think, his age some fifty, and his name is

John P. Gass;

Who respectfully says to his friends and the public, as that merry wag, Prince Hal, said to regal daddy, Henry IV., "Stay here and breathe awhile," even if for no other purpose than that of witnessing the improvements made, under his directions, to the well known EAGLE COFFEE-HOUSE; — a public establishment which, he does not hesitate to say, is, in comparison to others devoted to a similar purpose in New England, what the royal bird from whom it derives its name, is to the other tribes of the air.
The Traveler who has heretofore visited the Eagle, will, when he again views it, perceive that it has aroused itself, and now appears with extended *wings* and *feet;* for to the former large edifice, the present proprietor has added a *wing* of two stories, running back 75 feet; one other story to the *wing* in front; . . .

After explaining more details of his grand establishment, he goes on to call attention to his "124 elegant Feather Beds and Hair Matrasses, and other furniture of the most elegant and fashionable description."

Another similar statement that might well be made today when natural gas is being piped throughout the country is contained in this paragraph:

Almost every one at all conversant with the modern discoveries in Chemistry, is aware of the many useful purposes to which GAS

Courtesy of Elmer Munson Hunt

THE EAGLE COFFEE HOUSE IN CONCORD, NEW HAMPSHIRE SHOWING CONCORD COACH IN FOREGROUND.

In the Grecian Hall of this inn many events were held, including the coachmen's dance of 1839,

has been applied; but the individual who now addresses the public, is not informed that anyone, *save himself*, has hitherto availed himself of this important agent in carrying to perfection the art of COOKERY. He, however, in his exertions and anxiety to accommodate the taste, as well as the wants of the public, early discovered that a proper application of this substance to culinary delicacy of every viand submitted to its operation, over that to be, obtained by the ordinary processes of Kitchener, Glass, and other eminent gourmands. This circumstance alone, will, he flatters himself, secure him the patronage of the scientific world, as an offering to the efforts of *genius;* while his other accommodations will be found equally attractive to travellers generally.

The ever necessary bar of those days is described as "an object of Corinthian elegance," and followed by the warning not to make too frequent applications to its contents or else those who might follow the *Door*-ic instead of the Corinthian order, and mingle with the dust.

Alice Morse Earle in *Stage Coach and Tavern Days* gives one of the very few printed accounts of this Concord establishment and the balls held there. This paragraph reads:

In England the coachmen and coaches had an Annual Parade, a coaching day, upon the Royal Birthday, when coach-horses, coachmen and guards all were in gala attire. In America similar annual meetings were held in many vicinities. In Concord, New Hampshire, which was a great coaching center, an annual coaching parade was given in the afternoon and a "Stagemen's Ball" in the evening. "Knights of the whip" from New Hampshire and neighboring states attended this festival. The ball was held in the celebrated Grecian Hall — celebrated for its spring floor — which was built over the open carriage-houses and woodsheds attached to the Eagle Coffee-house, called now the Eagle Hotel. This dancing hall took its name from the style of its architecture. At one end was a great painting of the battle of New Orleans with Jackson on horseback. (Not particularly appropriate.) It was the rallying point for all great occasions — caucuses, conventions, concerts, even a six weeks' theatrical season.

Edward L. Bigelow, our President, loaned us a book called *The Nancy Flyer* which is a stagecoach novel containing much history on this subject. We have obtained permission from the author, Ernest Poole, to quote several sentences, and also part of the chapter on the Concord stage:

> The Coach Parade and Stagemen's Ball in Concord had been held each winter since back in 1829; and to it came Knights of the Whip from all over New Hampshire and neighbor states, men right up at the top of the game . . .

The "crew" of the "Flyer" including the wife and son came to town as the visiting drivers and friends were calling on Lewis Downing and his partner, Abbot, who stopped work in their shop to watch the parade:

> Picking up our women to join the rest in gay bonnets, hoods and furs in the line of coaches and sleighs, we formed behind the Fire Band and all pranced down Main Street, with jingling harness and flourish of horns . . . the ball was right there in the Grecian Hall, built over the Eagle coach sheds. Between the Greek columns at the sides hung lighted paper lanterns, garlands and festoons, and at one end was a great painting of Andrew Jackson on his horse in the Battle of New Orleans . . . I am no man to describe such things, but most of the drivers wore long pants fitting close to their shoes, tail coats and blue, red or yellow vests, while the women and girls had flowers and ribbons and bows of velvet in their hair, and dresses with skirts so big that in dancing they billowed out on the floor. Supper was sumptuous . . . for dancing the hall had a spring floor, and you could soon feel it rise and fall under the weight of a hundred and sixty couples of husky drivers and their daughters, sweethearts and wives, dancing polkas, waltzes, jigs and reels!

With the assistance of Edgar C. Hirst, President of the First National Bank of Concord, New Hampshire, and Elmer Munson Hunt, Director of the New Hampshire Historical Society, we have been fortunate in obtaining from the latter a number of references found in the newspapers of Concord. The earliest ball mentioned given by the stagedrivers of that and surrounding towns was on February 3, 1837, the glowing account in the *Patriot* reading:

Annual Stageman's Ball,

AT

Concord, N. H., Eagle Coffee House.

THE COMPANY OF

Mr. *Albert Herbert* and *Lady* is requested at the *Grecian Hall,* (*Wm. Walker & Son,*) on *Friday eve, Jan. 11, 1839.*

J. B. French,	Lowell, Mass.,		J. Barker,	Boston,
J. Newell,	Boston,		T. A. Staples,	do.
J. P. Stickney,	Concord, N H.,		W. Lawrence,	Nashua, N. H.,
A. Colby,	New London, N. H.,		G. Shepard,	Amherst, N. H.,
J. Gibson,	Francestown, N. H.,		D. R. Kimball,	Lowell, Mass ,
E. Brewer,	Barnet, Vt.,		R. G. Porter,	Nashua, N. H ,
J. Kelsey,	Danville. Vt.,		J. Conkey,	do.
J. Cady,	Lancaster, N. H.,		S. Dutton,	do.
L. A. Russell,	do.		W. A. Farewell,	do.
G. Bellows,	do.		B. Cheney,	do.
A. Haydon,	Montpelier, Vt.,		H. Rowbey,	Boston,
F. Pearl,	Haverhill, Mass.,	**Managers.**	R. Fisk,	do.
C. Hall,	do.		J. Gibbs,	Littleton, N. H.,
F. G. Whidden,	do.		W. B. French,	Rumney, N. H.,
D. Niles,	do.		J. F. Langdon,	do.
J. Mendum,	Portsmouth, N. H.		D. G. Fields,	Lyndon, Vt ,
S. Robinson,	do.		A. Fields,	do.
W. Barnaby,	do.		J. L. Dewey,	Hanover, N. H.,
E. Smith,	Haverhill. N. H.,		S. Smith,	do.
C. K. Lewis,	Lowell, Mass.,		S. Corbin.	Lowell, Mass.,
J. H. Elliott,	do.		A. Glidden,	Haverhill, N. H.,
A. Hagget,	do.		A. Palmer,	Derry, N H ,
D. Hoit,	Haverhill, Mass.,		J. D. Meserve,	Conway, N. H.,
T. Adams,	Salem, Mass.,		R. Morse,	Rumney, N. H ,
J. Haws,	Barnet. Vt.,		J. Peavey,	Tuftonborough, N. H.,
S. Meserve,	Lowell, Mass.,		E. Hutchins,	Concord, N. H ,
J. Smith,	Conway, N. H.,		W. Rodgers,	Danville. Vt ,
J. Gass,	Concord, N. H.,		R. Parker,	Lowell, Mass ,

MUSIC.

A. Pushee,	Lebanon, N. H.,
J. K. Kendall,	do.
E. Kendall,	Boston,
L. S. Sanborn,	do.
— Barrett,	do.
G. W. Post,	Lebanon, N. H,

Jan. 5, 1839.

Wm. White, Print.

Courtesy of Elmer Munson Hunt

INVITATION TO THE STAGEMAN'S BALL

Held in 1839 in the Grecian Hall of the Eagle Coffee House in Concord, New Hampshire, from the original in the New Hampshire Historical Society's Collection. No other invitation of this kind can be found.

The stagemen had a splendid Ball at the Eagle Coffee House in this town on the evening of Friday, last week. It was numerously attended, and embraced as many elegantly dressed and beautiful ladies, and hale goodlooking gentlemen as we have seldom seen collected on a similar occasion. The Governor was present and participated in the festivities of the occasion, as well as many others not of the profession. The music was superb, the entertainment excellent, and every thing went off much to the satisfaction of all concerned.

It would be interesting if a description had been handed down listing the various decorations connected with stagedriving that must have ornamented the walls at these parties, carrying out the scheme of decorations placed around the halls in which the Hunt Balls used to be held.

The following report appeared in the same newspaper on January 13, 1840:

The Stagemen's Ball, held at the Eagle Coffee House last Friday evening, was attended by one hundred and fifty couples, and every thing was done up in the neat and elegant style, peculiar to the gentlemen of the whip on such occasions. The entertainment provided by Walker was excellent, the music first rate, and the assembly of ladies brilliant.

On this occasion a certain Mr. Fuller sang a song composed by himself which it is related was received with much applause. A few verses are included here:

Old Shakespeare, who understood human affairs,
Said the world was a Stage and the people all players,
But I a new version will venture to broach
And for people read *Drivers*, for *Stage*, a *Stage Coach*.
　　Gee ho dobbin, gee ho dobbin, gee up and gee ho.

How manifest 'tis every person alive,
Who enters life's Coach has an itching to drive,
The Infant is striving to drive its mamma,
While she with a broom stick is driving papa.
　　Gee ho dobbin, gee ho dobbin, gee up and gee ho.

Of all the hard driving, the hardest I'm sure
The wretched old bachelor has to endure —
If on earth he would ever true happiness feel,
Let me tell him a wife's the main *spoke* in the *wheel*.

To those single females, who ardently strive,
Yet fear it's too late a good bargain to drive,
They're privileg'd surely now leap year prevails,
To make their *proposals* to *transport* the *Males*. (Mails)

And now, for a moment let's just take a glance,
To our drivers to-night, who have met here to dance;
On occasions like this, they're as ready to skip
As horses who jump at the crack of the whip.

May these yearly assemblies continue to thrive,
Good feelings and fellowship keeping alive,
Tho', occasional discords will visit all men
Next year may you all meet in Concord again.

To this magical circle of Beauty which fills
Our hearts with delight and true pleasure distills,
When the power of your charms we presume to withstand,
I hope the *Old Driver* will take us in hand.

Doubtless similar events took place almost every winter but apparently the only original invitation that can be found was loaned to us by Mr. Hunt and is reproduced herewith. The date is January 11, 1839. One of the managers was B. P. Cheney then a resident of Nashua, who began life as a stage driver, and in later life held large interests in many express and railroad companies, as told in another chapter, describing his remarkable career.

Short mentions were made of Annual Balls between the years 1845 and 1856, some taking place at the Washington Hotel but more frequently at the Eagle, the attendance varying from 76 to 175 couples.

The Historical Society also possesses a program of a "Cotillion Party" held at the Eagle Coffee House on December 28, 1838, a spread eagle surmounting the invitation. The event was scheduled to begin as early as five o'clock. It was not held primarily for stage drivers but doubtless a few of the "swellest" of their set took this opportunity to enjoy some relaxation after a hard day over the wintry roads. The Concord Coach at this party was, however, ably represented by Lewis Downing, the maker of these famous stages. No exciting incident, however, seems to have taken place, certainly compared to a celebrated cotillion in Boston whereat, according to the story told by a lady present, this curious incident took place. She told the writer that the only man she had ever seen the worse for wear was a certain person who came across the floor on all fours to ask her for a dance.

One of our office force, Miss Alice G. Higgins, has made a search in various local newspapers and has discovered an account of a stagemen's dance held in Haverhill, New Hampshire, about which the *Haverhill Republican* wrote "that the Stagemen's Ball which came off on the 13 inst. was a splendid affair, — dance, supper, and all connected therewith, reflecting much credit upon the 'Gentlemen of the Whip' and the host of the Exchange Hotel." This town was an important coaching center.

There is an account of a stagemen's Christmas dinner which runs as follows:

> It was a happy thought which brought two hundred and fifty "old stagers," of the Connecticut Valley, — Drivers, Proprietors and Agents, — together at Springfield for a merry Christmas in 1859. Hon. Ginery Twitchell and James Parker, Esq., of the Western Railroad, seem to have been promotors of this "gathering of the whips," and two days were given up to their entertainment in Springfield, during which the hospitalities of larder and stable were tested to the utmost.

A story connected with staging, found in the same paper, might well be brought in here.

As a yankee pedler of the genuine Connecticut breed was one day in front of a country tavern, watering a raw boned horse,

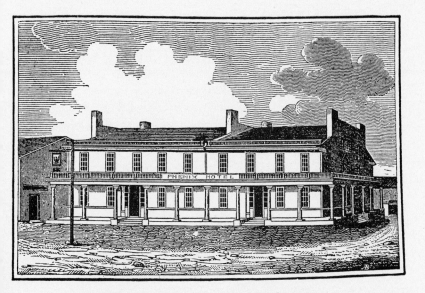

PHŒNIX HOTEL.

ABEL HUTCHINS,

CONCORD, NEW-HAMPSHIRE,

A FEW RODS SOUTH OF THE STATE-HOUSE,

INFORMS his Friends and the Public, that he has added, during the past summer, to his former accommodations, at the Sign of the

PHŒNIX HOTEL,

three new commodious PARLORS, and eighteen LODGING ROOMS, which will enable him to accommodate his customers with still more convenience than heretofore; and it will be his continual endeavor to render the PHŒNIX HOTEL a pleasant asylum for the Traveller, and an agreeable residence for the man of business or leisure.

Stages from Boston, Burlington, Vt. Stanstead, L. C. Haverhill and Hanover, arrive and depart every day, Sundays excepted;—from Portsmouth, Newburyport, Dover and Exeter, three times a week.

Stage Books kept for every Stage arriving in town.

MARCH, 1830.

Courtesy of Elmer Munson Hunt

whose ribs might be as easily counted as marbles in a boy's pocket, a roguish looking horse jockey, accosted the pedler, thinking to have some fun with him as follows:

"I say, I rather imagine it don't cost much to keep that creature in feed, does it?"

"Wal now, what would you give to know! I make it a rule never to trade for nothin."

"Well," said the jockey "if you can feed him on anything cheaper than laths and brickbats, and support life, I'll treat."

"Done!" said Jonathan putting both hands into his pockets and looking up into the jockey's face, "I'll take yer up, stranger, I just gets a lot of shavings and a pair of green spectacles on the animal's nose, and the foolish creature thinks it's grass! At that rate he eats a barrel a day! Now stranger, I'll take a sweetner, if you please."

The Presidential Ball of February 22, 1849 held at The Depot Hotel in Concord, New Hampshire was evidently a grand affair. Cuts of Taylor and Fillmore appear on the invitation, surrounded by the American Eagle and flags of our country. The entreating headline reads, "Sir, Your Company, with Ladies, is respectfully solicited." Again the distinguished Downing family, father and son, of whom much is told in another chapter, assisted as Manager and on the Committee of Arrangements respectively.

Albert Herbert apparently was a social leader in Concord as his name is written in on the back of some of the programs in the Historical Society Collections. Perhaps he may have held the same position of prominence in the events of the New Hampshire town that several of Boston's distinguished citizens held as leaders of most of our Cotillions here, when no ball was complete without their presence.

It is a pity more could not be learned about these unique stage drivers' events. Nevertheless, it does not require much imagination to visualize the burly and perhaps roughly dressed driver rigged out in his "very best" dancing with his girl friend dressed in all the finery she could muster up for the occasion.

BUFFALO BILL AND HIS FAMOUS
DEADWOOD STAGECOACH

ALMOST EVERYONE, except those of the most recent generations, has seen this "Deadwood" coach at Buffalo Bill's Wild West Show, taking the most prominent part in a scene in which it was "attacked" by real but friendly Indians and then "rescued" by "brave" cowboys, led by Buffalo Bill. The story of this world-famous stagecoach was well told by Elmer Munson Hunt in a publication of The New Hampshire Historical Society of which he is a director and by several other well-posted authors. It is included here as it was built by the Abbot-Downing Company of Concord, New Hampshire in the year 1863 under the personal supervision of Lewis Downing, Jr., the President. The "Deadwood" coach was shipped the following year around the Horn in the clipper *General Grant* to San Francisco, where it became the property of the Pioneer Stage Company of California. Its first assignment was to carry passengers and mails for a long time to and from the gold mines in Northern California. An amusing account in the *Kansas Historical Quarterly* gives a description of the departure of this stage from Leavenworth for the mines:

> A crowd gathered in front of the Planters' House to see our equipages start. Amid confused ejaculations of "Good bye, old boy," "Write as soon as you get there," "Better have your hair cut so the Arapahoes can't scalp you," "Tell John to send me an ounce of dust," "Be sure and give Smith that letter from his wife," "Do write the facts about gold," the whips cracked and the two stages rolled merrily away.

From this peaceful, though monotonous existence, the Deadwood stage was soon transferred to duty in dangerous work on the plains, where it encountered the fire of Indians and brigands. It was then taken across the Sierras to the Rockies, whereupon it was used in Wyoming during the lively days of staging in the town of Deadwood, whence it got its name. This town was then

DEADWOOD
CHAMBER of
COMMERCE

Courtesy of Nell Perrigoue, Secretary, Deadwood Chamber of Commerce

This Illustration Shows A Concord Coach
as it Appears on The Letterhead of
the Chamber of Commerce of
The Town of Deadwood, South Dakota

The formation in the background represents one of the many
Cambrian, or pre-Cambrian, outcroppings within the city limits
of Deadwood.

described as "The raw, roaring capital of the Black Hills mining camp." Today it is a progressive and thriving place, described by the Deadwood Chamber of Commerce as "the most vividly Western town that ever sprang up along a placer stream." This has reference, of course, to the mining craze that brought scores of fortune seekers to the town. The well-known Homestake Mine is only a few miles away. Probably Concord coaches ran to this mine, but Donald H. McLaughlin, President of the Company, writes that the early records were lost in a fire.

The Deadwood coach, nevertheless, survived many severe attacks, and the Concord *Monitor*, referring to its career on the plains wrote:

In the day of its prosperity, glistening with new paint and varnish, bedecked with gold leaf, every strap new and shining, it traversed the most deadly mail route in the west from Cheyenne to Deadwood, via Laramie, and through a country alive with the banditti of the plains.

The route lay through a country of picturesque nomenclature and of extreme peril. In its first season the dangerous places on the route were Buffalo Gap, Lame Johnny Creek, Red Canyon and Squaw Gap, all of which were made famous by scenes of slaughter and the deviltry of the highwaymen.

Agnes Wright Spring in her account of *The Cheyenne and Black Hills Stage and Express Routes* recounted that:

Dave Dickey, skilled reinsman, was on the boot of the first Deadwood stage. He proudly sent his well-matched six-horse outfit rocking down the long narrow gulch that was fringed by gambling rooms, stores, dance halls, and barrooms. And when the wheels ground to a stop in front of the stage office, loud cheers went up from the miners who swarmed around the coach.

E. C. Bent, described as "a young and popular Cheyenne medicine man," who had been appointed stage agent, was on hand to receive the first cargo.

Being ambitious, the owners then fitted the stage up as a treasure coach, and of course, the highwaymen and Indians at once became very much interested. The coach was defended by what were known as "shot gun messengers." Thereupon many deadly conflicts ensued and at one time, when the driver was killed, a woman called Martha Jane Canary, known on the frontier as "Calamity Jane," an unusual character of the town of Deadwood, grabbed the reins and saved the coach and its valuable contents. "Calamity Jane," so named because she was such a good person to have around in time of calamity, had so many good qualities that her name is remembered, along with other early characters, in the yearly parade held in Deadwood each summer to recall the frontier days of 1876. Those early years of encounters with the Indians are kept alive in the unique name of the *Tomahawk Country Club*.

On one occasion the sum of sixty thousand dollars was captured by raiders, and at another time the Sioux Indians made a terrific but unsuccessful attack upon the Deadwood coach. Some while later, in 1876, Buffalo Bill is said to have returned in this same coach from a scouting expedition, carrying with him the scalps of several of the Indians he and his men had encountered. How many other stories this vehicle could have told!

Some months afterwards, the Deadwood stagecoach was again attacked and captured by highwaymen and left in a deserted canyon somewhere in the heart of the Rockies, there, presumably, to spend its last days. This was not to be, however, for Colonel Cody by good luck heard of its whereabouts and organized a party to recapture it. With delight it was brought into camp, and later it filled a major role in most of his Wild West shows, so vividly described by Richard J. Walsh in his *The Making of Buffalo Bill:*

> Thunder of hoofs, clank of spurs, rattle of wheels, swish of lariat and crack of rifles, glint of shattered glass balls, odors of gunpowder and cattle, made it authentic and amazing. It began with a bareback pony race between Indians and went on to its climax with a "grand realistic battle scene depicting the capture, torture and death of a scout by the savages, the revenge, recapture of the dead body and victory of the cowboys and government scouts." Cowboys rode the bucking broncoes, roped and tied the Texas steers, lassoed and rode the wild bison. A fleet-footed Indian ran a race with a mounted rival. The pony express rider dashed in, changed his mochila to a fresh mount and dashed off again. The "startling and soul-stirring attack on the Deadwood mail coach" ended in a rescue by scouts led by Cody and Carver.

As another writer expressed it, this coach now "played a different role from that of inviting murder and being the tomb of its passengers." Early in its career a rival show-man procured another stage of his own to which he gave the name of "Deadwood," but the original held sway for many years to come.

The second chapter in the long history of this Concord-made vehicle enumerates briefly its appearances in many towns throughout the United States. A friend of Cody's advised him to take the show east and give the "tenderfeet" a real taste of Western life. One of the stopping places was at Omaha, whence it wended its way to a five weeks' run at Coney Island, New York.

The arrival in Boston was well written up by Walsh:

Six weeks after he left the Platte River Cody was astonishing
sedate Boston by the skill with which he drove his strange cavalcade of wagons, buffalo, elk, steers, mules, ponies and Indians
through the narrow curves of Washington Street.

Of the visit to fashionable Newport the same writer had
an amusing story:

The "upper ten" of Newport society turned out among the
ten thousand people who filled the Aquidneck Fair Grounds in
mid-July. Lord Mandeville became the lion of the day by volun-
teering to be a passenger in the Deadwood coach during the
pursuit by Indians, and by swooning dramatically as if wounded.
"Half a dozen cowboys sprang to the coach door and tenderly
brought the Duke of Manchester's son and heir out and conveyed
him carefully to the judge's stand, where he was tended by loving
hands, beneath the influence of which he speedily recovered."

There were many internal difficulties but the show was re-
organized and continued on its way, the factory No. 150 coach
built by the Abbot-Downing Company still figuring as the great
attraction, which a good many of us have seen and remember.
One of the regular passengers was John Nelson who was married
to an Indian and for many years "his whiskers were to float in
the breeze as he sat on the top of the careening Deadwood
coach," to quote an authority. The following season one of the
ads read, "A Year's Visit West in Three Hours." Over forty
thousand persons saw the exhibition in Chicago in one day and
then the cavalcade, in 1884, journeyed to New York. The coach,
drawn by six horses, was reported as passing along Fifth Avenue
on Sunday morning, much to the churchgoers' surprise. Continuing, the article describes Buffalo Bill and others clinging to
the narrow seats on top as the procession wended its way to the
Polo Grounds. The report of the show referred especially to the
cowboys lassoing steers and to Bill Cody chasing buffaloes around
the course, adding that "Indians attacked the stagecoach which
was lighted inside by red fire to convey the impression that the
passengers were being burned to death."

*Photographed from a program of the Wild West Show in the
New York Public Library
Courtesy of Paul H. Downing*

The Deadwood Coach Being Attacked by "Indians" and
"Rescued" by Cowboys, in Buffalo Bill's Wild West Show

It was decided in December to take the exhibition to New
Orleans and a boat was chartered for the long voyage down
river. On the way, unfortunately, bad luck met them and almost
all the animals, except a few horses, were drowned. Good fortune, however, followed our Deadwood Coach and in some
extraordinary manner it was saved by great effort and ingenuity.
A performance was quickly gotten together and the stage as
usual played its important part, but before very poor houses.

Returning north, the well-known "Little Sure-Shot" —
Annie Oakley, (in Indian dialect "Watanga Cicilia") then
nineteen years of age, joined the troupe and when she was not
shooting glass balls, she must have sometimes ridden in the old
stage.

Let us digress for a moment and recall a few of the high-
lights of this greatest of women rifle shots, who began at a very
early age to shoot game in order to supply her family with food.
Many curious honors and requests awaited her, almost as many

as Buffalo Bill himself received. We will mention several only. The Grand Duke of Russia, a great shot, succumbed to her prowess in a shooting competition in London and in Paris President Carnot actually offered her a commission in the French Army; the Shah of Persia and the Sultan of Turkey were much struck with her humble manners and her wonderful performances in Paris; and to cap the climax, the King of Senegal offered to buy her to defend his villages from man-eating tigers. Will Rogers summed her up in these words: "She was just about the most perfect thing you ever saw besides your mother."

Canada was also visited and at one time while there a lasso expert pulled off a tall hat worn by one of the Aldermen sitting in the grandstand.

"I'm as happy as the sun!" said Buffalo Bill as twenty-five thousand persons began flocking into the show grounds. "Such a sight is enough to make any man a laughing hyena with happiness." A successful summer on Staten Island, bringing spectators back and forth in seventeen steam boats, and an equally good winter in Madison Square Garden decided the show officials to try their luck in Europe to show the people over there our real western life. This gigantic undertaking set sail on the *State of Nebraska* on March 31, or April 1, 1887. It must have resembled Noah's Ark, but we're quite sure there was no cowboy band in the Ark to play "The Girl I Left Behind Me."

"From Prairie to Palace" was used as the heading of a chapter describing the meeting of Bill Cody and many heads of Royal families in England and on the Continent, which provided the material for the final part of this article. It was a daring venture to carry the immense show to Europe and set it up in the center of West End London for its performances. Before the official opening the Prince and Princess of Wales came to see what a Wild West show looked like and carried back the report that it was wonderful. Queen Victoria, then celebrating her Golden Jubilee, at once sent a "command" that the show be put on in one hour, and Buffalo Bill said to himself, "Cody, you've

THE DEADWOOD MAIL — MOST FAMOUS VEHICLE IN THE WORLD

From a folder issued by Abbot-Downing Company   :   *Courtesy of Mrs. E. R. Shaw, Nashua, N. H.*

THIS FAMOUS STAGECOACH RETURNED TO CONCORD, NEW HAMPSHIRE IN 1895, DRIVEN BY "BUFFALO BILL"

It was built by the Abbot-Downing Co. of Concord in 1863 and was shown by Colonel Cody in most of his Wild West shows in this country and abroad. Its adventures are mentioned in several chapters, including Queen Victoria's visit to Buffalo Bill, and *Punch's* amusing account of the Wild West performance.

fetched 'em.'' It was stated that for the first time since the Declaration of Independence "a sovereign of Great Britain saluted the Star Spangled Banner — and that banner was carried by Buffalo Bill,'' as he rode around the ring and saluted the Queen in her specially prepared box. Buffalo Bill, Annie Oakley, the Sioux Chief, a tiny papoose and others were presented to the Queen, and according to Thomas Archer's *Life and Jubilee of Queen Victoria*, the Deadwood Coach was still one of the greatest attractions as it was attacked by the Indians who were, as usual, repelled by the cowboys.

From the story of Queen Victoria as told by Archer, we get a detailed account of her attendance at the "Wild West" show when it made this visit to London in June of 1887, "The Queen," according to this authority, "having some curiosity to see the remarkable exhibition called the 'Wild West,' in which Indians, 'Cowboys,' Californians and others went through performances illustrative of Indian and prairie life under the direction of Colonel W. F. Cody (popularly called 'Buffalo Bill')." Continuing, he wrote:

> The performances here — the display of horsemanship, of Indian, Mexican, and Cowboy racing, of skilled rifle-shooting by two young ladies of California, and of various picturesque feats and scenes, including the attacks by Indians on the Deadwood Coach and the isolated hut on an imaginary ranch, and their repulse by the Cowboys — had for some days been attracting half the world of fashion in London.

A newspaper clipping from the *Omaha Bee*, in the Abbot-Downing record book, described this unique event under the heading:

COL. CODY AND THE QUEEN.
THE GREAT SCOUT ENTERTAINED THE
LATE QUEEN VICTORIA IN LONDON.

The clipping contained also these paragraphs:

> A Nebraskan it was who gave Queen Victoria the only glimpse she ever had of that phase of American life which existed in such

abundance during much of her reign and marked the transformation of primeval wastes into a domain excelling her own.

. . .

It was on a June day in 1887, less than a week prior to the celebration of her golden jubilee, that England's foremost woman was handed from her carriage to a sumptuously furnished box in a great amphitheatre at Earl's Court, London, and there for two hours was the guest of Colonel William F. Cody — Nebraska's "Buffalo Bill" — and the Wild West show.

. . .

The performance was almost identical with those given in this country before and since, but it was all new and a revelation to the queen . . .

After the performance, at her own request, a little papoose that had figured in one of the Indian scenes was brought to her box and she entertained him in a way that the benighted little beggar did not seem at all to appreciate, albeit she was gentle.

Colonel Cody was now out of debt and the box office was doing well. There exist photographs of the Redskin Village set up in London during their stay.

The most influential men and women of England, including Gladstone and his wife, visited the show. Soon a second performance was desired by Queen Victoria for the entertainment of her Royal guests who had journeyed from many countries to attend her Golden Jubilee, three hundred in all, counting the wives, children and retainers. "There was one gorgeous feat of publicity," wrote Richard Walsh:

The old Deadwood coach, as it was chased under fire by Indians, held four crowned heads, ducking slightly, while the Prince of Wales clung on the driver's box. To perpetuate the publicity an anecdote was told and retold for many years. The Prince of Wales remarked, "Colonel, you never held four kings like these, did you?" ("For," Cody would say, "I had taught him the great American game of draw poker.") Cody's pat reply was: "I've held four kings, but four kings and the Prince of Wales makes a royal flush, and that's unprecedented." The joke was obscure to the four kings in the coach. "I almost pitied Wales when he tried to explain in three languages."

At one time the Princess, herself, insisted upon riding around the ring in the old coach, and apropos of this incident, during their sojourn in London a letter was received from General Sherman, part of which we quote:

Fifth Avenue Hotel,
New York, June 29, 1887.

Hon. Wm. F. Cody,
London, England

Dear Cody: * * * In common with all your countrymen, I want to let you know that I am not only gratified, but proud of your management and general behavior; so far as I can make out, you have been modest, graceful, and dignified in all you have done to illustrate the history of civilization on this continent during the past century.

I am especially pleased with the graceful and pretty compliment paid you by the Princess of Wales, who rode in the Deadwood coach while it was attacked by the Indians and rescued by the cowboys. Such things did occur in our days, and may never again.

As near as I can estimate, there were in 1865 *about nine and a half millions of buffaloes* on the plains between the Missouri River and the Rocky Mountains. All are now gone — killed for their meat, their skins and bones.

This seems like desecration, cruelty, and murder, yet they have been replaced by twice as many *neat* cattle. At that date there were about 165,000 *Pawnees, Sioux, Cheyennes, Kiowas* and *Arapahoes*, who depended on these buffaloes for their yearly food. They, too, are gone . . . . . .

W. T. Sherman

The name "Buffalo Bill" was of course given Cody for his skill in rounding up herds of buffaloes and killing them one by one as he circled around the outside. Within seventeen months he had made away with 4,280 and a short piece of poetry seemed to lead to the reason for his name:

Buffalo Bill, Buffalo Bill,
Never missed and never will;
Always aims and shoots to kill
And the company pays his buffalo bill.

On the Deadwood stage he was equally at home and a friend of his once said he was the only man he ever saw who could sit on the box and hit all four of his horses with one motion.

This typical plainsman now became the "lion" of London. Invitations came in quick order, and in return the head of the show provided his guests with Indian meals, said to have been cooked in the open and eaten with the fingers. At a meeting of the London Coaching Club he had the box seat with Lord Beresford, quite a different appearing coach from the old Dead-wood stage! Annie Oakley shared honors; she appeared at gun clubs and women took shooting lessons from her. The Prince of Wales presented her with a medal and photographs were exchanged.

Although Colonel Cody was so well received wherever he visited, he did not fare as well at one of Boston's exclusive clubs. During his stay here he was put up by an influential member familiar with the West, who was requested to withdraw his name. One wonders if the Election Committee feared that Buffalo Bill and his crack shot, Annie Oakley, might shoot up the pictures on the walls or possibly even scalp some of the members themselves, provided they could find any members who had hair enough to catch a good hold on!

One has often wondered why most Indian scouts and fighters grew their hair so long, and it will interest those of our time to know a reason given by a writer on Western life:

***Cody went to visit his family, who during his long absence had been staying at St. Louis. His appearance was a shock to his wife. He wore a long mustache, a tiny goatee and hair strag-gling toward his shoulders.

"What on earth did you grow it for?" she cried.

"Why, I had to," he explained. "It's the fashion out West now. You're not a regular scout unless you've got this sort of rigout."

This was true. It had become a point of honor with all who must fight the Indians to let the hair grow long enough to form a respectable scalp-lock, so that if one should be so unfortunate as to fall in the fight, the savage might not be cheated of the scalp.

To cut the hair short was to be a coward; to let it grow was to display sportsmanship and proclaim defiance. Custer did it, and Wild Bill, and Cody followed their example.

On one occasion, if you believe it, Cody was so proud of the scalp that he took from his great enemy, Yellow Hand, that after carrying it in his pocket several weeks he packed it carefully in a box and shipped it to his wife. He then had to make her a promise he would never do that again and it is said that this was the last trophy of this nature he acquired.

There is a song of the Black Hills of South Dakota often sung by the drivers, scouts and prospectors in Deadwood, which ends with the mention of scalping:

> For old Sitting Bull or Comanche Bills
> We'll lift off your hair in the dreary Black Hills.

There is another tale related of Cody and his spouse. It must be admitted that at certain times during his long and varied career he resorted to a good deal of "strong water." A story is related that he returned home sober and requested his wife to let him in. "No," she replied, "I know that isn't you from the different tone of your voice." He thereupon went back to camp and had a few drinks with his scout friends. When he returned home he again appealed for permission to enter his abode, whereupon his wife said "I know that is you Bill, come in." It should be added that on his many journeys with his show he always behaved in a very gentlemanly way.

It has been stated that two and a half million people visited the show during its stay in London.

The troupe came home on the *Persian Monarch*, debarking as the band played *Yankee Doodle*.

Cody was ambitious and so a second European tour was planned in the spring of 1889. Going aboard amid a severe rain, the account said that the buffaloes, cowboys and Indians were soaked. Even the old Deadwood coach, it is reported, "stood on the deck leaking at every crevice until pools of water soaked its sacred cushions." Landing at Le Havre, they played to Paris crowds with great success. Relics from the West sold in the shops and cowboys and Indians were seen riding in the Bois. Then they moved to Spain, Italy, Austria-Hungary and Germany. Barcelona didn't treat the show as well as it did Columbus on his return from his epochal voyage, for typhoid and influenza raged and seven Indians succumbed.

The Coliseum in Rome was too small for the exhibit, but it brought forth, nevertheless, these few lines:

> I'll take my stalwart Indian braves
> Down to the Coliseum,
> And the old Romans from their graves
> Will all arise to see 'em.
> Prepare triumphal cars for me,
> And purple thrones to sit on,
> For I've done more than Julius C---

Before Mt. Vesuvius Buffalo Bill staged a war dance and there are pictures of him and some of his Indians "doing" Venice in a gondola. Then Pope Leo XIII was paid a visit by the whole troupe on the anniversary of his coronation.

An amusing anecdote is well told by Walsh relative to Annie Oakley's visit to Germany:

How Annie might have prevented the World War became the subject of anecdote and cartoon. One day in Berlin William Hohenzollern saw her shoot the ashes from a cigarette held in a man's mouth. He asked her to try it on him. She did so, clipping the end of his cigar. "Annie missed the Kaiser by about four inches," her husband said. The sequel is that in 1917 she sat down and wrote the Kaiser a letter asking for another shot at him.

Belgium was not forgotten. The spring of 1892 saw the show again in London and a command performance was held at Windsor Castle. The *Omaha Bee* again printed an account of this meeting:

In 1892, upon the show's second visit to England, she [Queen Victoria] had the whole performance repeated on the Windsor lawn for the entertainment of a large party, and it was on this occasion that she presented the Colonel the diamond brooch. . . . The prince did not participate, but the princess rode on the seat

of the stage with Fred Mathews, the driver, and later spent a half
hour in Annie Oakley's tent. . . . It was after these merry occasions, stultified by so little formality, that Colonel Cody entertained them all in the show's cook tent at a typical American
dinner of the plainsman's day. . . .

An English cousin of the writer, Mrs. Peter Vanneck,
obtained through Sir Owen Morshead, Librarian of Windsor
Castle, permission to print an extract from Queen Victoria's
diary describing her viewing of the Wild West Show:

1892

June 25. Windsor Castle. . . . At 5 we went on to the East Terrace,
& watched from a tent, open in front, a sort of "Buffalo Bill"
performance, on the Lawn below. It was extremely well arranged,
& an excellent representation of what we had also seen 5 years ago
at Earl's Court. There were Cow Boys, Red Indians, Mexicans,
Argentinos, taking part, & then a wonderful riding display by
Cossacks, accompanied by curious singing, & a war dance by the
Indians. There were extraordinary buck jumping horses, shooting
at glass balls, by Col. Cody (Buffalo Bill), & display of cracking
huge long whips. The whole, was a very pretty wild sight, which
lasted an hour. At the conclusion of the performance, all advanced
in line at a gallop & stopped suddenly. Col. Cody was brought
up for me to speak to him. He is still a very handsome man, but
has now got a grey beard. . . .

The Deadwood coach of course participated in the performance
as usual.

For a few years the show continued abroad but had many
ups and downs. The original Deadwood coach held together
until about the year 1898 when it had to be discarded and
replaced by a new one, but the former made one more visit
back to Concord, New Hampshire, on July 4, 1895. This has
been described as the most romantic, though not the most exciting episode in the long life of the Deadwood Stage. Buffalo
Bill, who usually sat on the driver's seat during his tours of two
continents, handled the reigns himself on this eventful day. Lewis
Downing was no longer living at that time but his son, Lewis
Downing, Jr., met Col. Cody and rode in the parade that

THE DEADWOOD COACH

Showing Buffalo Bill, and on top one of his crack drivers. The coach was built in Concord, New Hampshire in 1863; it carried many of royal birth and many distinguished Americans, while Col. Cody's "Wild West Show" was appearing abroad. Search has been made in vain for the original Deadwood coach, and it is presumed that it no longer exists.

day inside the coach, with Buffalo Bill on the box driving a team of six mules. In the coach with Downing was Hiram Rolfe, successor to John Burgum, Abbot-Downing's foreman painter who had served the Company for fifty-two years compared with Mr. Downing's fifty-eight, making a total of one hundred and ten years. Buffalo Bill also staged a Wild West show in Concord before twenty thousand persons. The *Monitor* of Concord, referring to the coach, spoke of "the battered sides, the paintless panels, the missing boot, its rusty iron, which were eloquent of hard knocks."

There is a picture in this chapter showing the coach and Buffalo Bill. The Deadwood Coach, now enjoying a well-earned rest, somewhere, has often been termed the most famous vehicle in the world.

As for Cody himself, he received the Congressional Medal of Honor, was chosen to the Nebraska Legislature and also was appointed Judge Advocate General of Wyoming; he was even talked of as a possibility for Vice President of the United States and, of interest to the subject of this booklet, it is said he even kept a tavern for a time.

His death occurred in Denver, Colorado, on January 10, 1917 and he was buried a short distance south of Golden, Colorado, near State Highway No. 68, about twenty miles from Denver. On June 3, 1917, with impressive ceremonies, his body was moved to a tomb blasted from solid rock on the highest point of Lookout Mountain (7,375 feet). The lodge near the foot of the mountain contains many interesting relics pertaining to his career. Cody made a great deal of money with his Wild West show but knew little about management of property and lost a large part of the fortune he accumulated. He invested heavily in land in Nebraska and Wyoming. In the latter State he founded a village named for him at the eastern entrance to Yellowstone Park. Cody, Wyoming, was incorporated as a town in 1900 and now has a Buffalo Bill Museum and a monument to perpetuate the memory of its founder.

"PUNCH" GOES TO THE WILD WEST SHOW

These passages and pictures from *Punch* at the time of Buffalo
Bill's Wild West Show in London in the spring of 1887 are reproduced by kind permission of Alan G. Agnew, Managing Director
of that magazine. Assistance to this end was given us by Sir Evelyn
Wrench, Editor of *The Spectator* and by E. D. W. Chaplin, its
Managing Director. Credit also should be given to the London
office of the English-Speaking Union which, through Barbara
Bonner, Librarian, called to our attention that *Punch* had printed
a number of articles concerning Buffalo Bill in its issues at that
time.

THE EXTENT of the interest aroused in England by Buffalo Bill's
Wild West Show in 1887 is shown by the wide publicity given to
it and also by the large attendance. We have found that *Punch*
contained a number of especially interesting and amusing
articles, several of which were contributed by its correspondent
"Robert."

Whether "Mr. Punch" himself had a ride at Windsor
Castle in the Deadwood Coach we do not know, but we do find
mention of this noted Concord (New Hampshire) built vehicle
in an amusing account under the heading "With the Indians on
the Derby Day." (June 4, 1887) Most of this article is here
quoted:

For many weeks past, go where I will, I have been unable to
escape from a variety of highly and biliously coloured advertise-
ment-pictures of savage Indians and picturesque persons in sort
of Mexican hunter's costume, riding recklessly among prairies,
shooting everything and everybody — and of other gallant sports-
men, riding wild buffaloes or bisons, which were represented by
the artist as uncommonly spirited animals, all of them like "Old
Jo" in the song, "kicking up ahind and afore."

Besides these, I had been haunted by the portrait of the leader
of the troupe, Buffalo Bill himself, who is represented as a sort of
wild Tennyson, of thirty or forty years ago, with a moustache, and

Reproduced by permission of PUNCH, Alan S. Agnew, Managing Director

This amusing caricature was inspired by the bucking broncos that appeared in Buffalo Bill's Wild West Show in London during the spring of 1887.

a fixed stony stare, suggestive of wool-gathering, which, by the way, may account for the length of his flowing locks. I had heard that Buffalo Bill, in private, was the Hon. Something Cody, American Senator, who preferred this style of sporting Showman's life to attending in his place in Congress, — just as if Mr. Gladstone led away by his enthusiastic passion for tree-chopping, should chuck up his Parliamentary career, let his hair grow long, assume a picturesque dress, and make a tour of the world, on his own axes, with a company illustrating English life at Hawarden, and calling himself "Woodchopping Will," . . .

I was told that Buffalo Bill's Show at Earl's Court gave a vivid and truthful representation of Life in the Far West — that is a West much farther than Kensington. And so, ever anxious to complete a neglected education, and, from my youth upward, devotedly attached to the novels of Fenimore Cooper, it occurred to me that the Derby Day offered a chance of seeing Buffalo Bill's Show in comparative quiet. I don't know to what temperature the Noble Savages and the Cowboys and Cowgirls are accustomed, but on this occasion, the unfortunate spectators in the two-shilling seats, who could not careen about, sat in the most piercing draughts that the Wild North-East could provide, a few protecting themselves with huddling together underneath their umbrellas (I personally huddled) while others were turning up their coat-collars, and regretting the absence of wraps. If the weather continues like this, a good trade might be done by the programme-sellers at Buffalo Bill's in hot-water bottles and foot-warmers.

From what I saw there, I gather that Life in the Wild West is a theatrical, circus-like sort of existence; . . . that Noble Savages ride in at full gallop to the accompaniment of airs from La Grande Duchesse, and other popular tunes, that they swoop and whoop, and squeak and shriek, in all the bravery of their paint and feathers; and that this, as far as I could understand it, is the only "bravery" they display, as there is nothing particularly daring in coming out, some forty or fifty of them, to attack four harmless travellers riding in a tumble-down old ramshackle vehicle — well named the "Dead-wood Coach" — and, on the appearance of Buffalo Bill and the Cowboys, to gallop away again in abject terror. Nor is it remarkably courageous for the same number of savages, representing the entire tribe, to come out to steal a solitary horse which is quietly grazing on the sawdust plain in front of a log-hut where a man and his wife and a chance traveller, the owner of the aforesaid horse, are taking a little refreshment, with the blinds down. Two Indian scouts stealthily approach the horse, one appropriates it, and the other, in burglarious fashion, climbs on to the roof of the log-hut in order to shoot anyone coming out at the door, which he could have done just as well if he had remained, like a sort of Indian *Chery Slyme,* "round the corner," without taking this extra trouble. In the meantime "the Braves" are in ambush behind some property trees and rocks. Suddenly, bang go rifles, the Cowboys, headed by Buffalo Bill, appear; more wild banging; the Indians ride round and round, and, with screams and shouts and more war-whooping, scuttle off as hard as they can in the direction of the painted trees and rocks, behind which is their encampment. In fact, whenever the Noble Savages come into collision with the Cowboys, they get the worst of it.

But is this the true story of Wild West life? Why should the Noble Savage be always beaten by the Cowboys? It is a fight between Cowboys and Cow-ards. One day the Indians will turn sulky, and refuse to play any more, unless the Cowboys agree to be alternately the defeated party.

. . . The Honble. Cody, who, as Buffalo Bill, doesn't do much except career about, take off his hat gracefully, and shoot at glass balls, which, though clever, is not quite a novelty. . . .

The buck-jumping is the only thing that doesn't seem to me to smell of the footlights and sawdust. It is a decidedly exciting, and really dangerous performance. It struck me that the "Wild West" on the cold, Northeasterly Derby Day, seemed to be rather a Tame West, the depression being, perhaps, attributable to a natural feeling of resentment on the part of the Cowboys and Indians at being kept at work instead of being taken for a holiday to see the Derby. But B.B. knows best; and if the Noble Savages had once got a sniff of freedom and the fresh air of the Downs, they might have gone for a lark all over Surrey, have attacked the Dorking Coach, driven the donkey-boys off the sands of Margate, won all the nuts at shooting, scalped the Nigger Minstrels, frightened the Nurserymaids, seized the bathing-machines, and used them as an encampment on the plains of Thanet . . . Only one word in the Honble. Cody's ear, — I should let the Indians win now and then, just for a treat. Also, what's the use of that gallant sportsman who ascends a pulpit and makes continual harangues, presumably descriptive of the Show, but scarcely one word of which could I, or those about me, catch on that lamentably cold Derby Day? I hope somebody hears him, as otherwise, if he is doing this twice every day, he is rather wasting his sweetness on the desert air of Tame West Kensington.

With this story is also a cut showing the reverse of one of the acts — an Indian on horseback with tomahawk raised, chasing Buffalo Bill.

The May 21, 1887, edition of *Punch* prints this piece of poetry to the rhythm of Hiawatha under the title of "The Song of Punchiwatha:"

THE QUEEN AT THE WILD WEST.
Would you hear how Colonel Cody
Gave his wondrous exhibition.
Of his Indians on the war-path,
In the sight of Queen Victoria:

Listen to this simple story
From the mouth of Punchiwatha.

When she reached the Exhibition,
Lo! a box near the arena
Was prepared for her reception:
Whitley too and Colonel Russell
And the wily Townsend Percy
As an escort to the lady,
To the Empress of the North Land.
Then the Indians and the Cowboys,
And the wonderful Vaqueros,
Raced and charged and whirled before her,
Stopped the coach, and wheeled and circled,
Like some birds of brilliant plumage
Round a carcase on the mountains.
Balls of glass were thrown and shattered
By the clever Colonel Cody,
Like Wabe-no the magician;
Ladies, too, there wielded rifles
Even as the strong man Kwa-sind.

To the Queen came Ogila-Sa,
Sioux Chief, and bowed before her;
He across the Big-Sea-Water
Came to see the Queen and Empress,
And will tell the wondrous story
Oft times in the Wild West wigwams,
In the days of the Hereafter.

To the Queen too, the papooses,
Dusky little Indian babies,
Were presented, and she touched them
Gently with a royal finger;
That the squaws, the happy mothers,
Might go back upon Kee-way-din,
On the Home-Wind o'er the water,
To the land of the Ojibways,
To the land of the Dacotahs,
To the Mountains of the Prairie,
Singing gaily all the praises
Of the gentle Queen and Empress,
And the wonders of the North Land.

Another article in this same number refers to Queen Victoria's attendance at the show:

THE VERY PLACE. — Why did the QUEEN go for a private view to B. B.'s in Wild West Kensington, when HER MAJESTY could have commanded the buck-jumping riders to have given their show at Buckingham Palace? Then the QUEEN, in bestowing *largesse* on the tame Wild Indians and Cowboys, could Shakespearingly have said, "So much for buck-jumping-'em."

Henley, too, is brought in with a pun relative to sculls and scalping:

THE Wild West Indians were not permitted to go to Henley last week. It was thought that the sight of so many sculls would be too much for them, and that they would immediately want to scalp everybody. Why doesn't the Honourable Colonel Buffalo Bill engage "Squash," and give him a show on a buck-jumper?

Still another reference is made to Her Majesty:

From all accounts, it appears that Her Majesty need not have gone to West Kensington to witness a war-dance of Wild Indians, as the Dowagers of her own Buckingham Palace, in their paint and feathers, could have provided her with a much fiercer and more savage entertainment on the spot, on a recent occasion. Duelling will come in fashion for ladies if this sort of thing is allowed, and a Drawing-Room will be worse than the House in debate on the Irish Crimes Bill.

The Military Tournament took place at this time and *Punch* lays particular emphasis on its success as compared to Bill Cody's exhibition.

A page in the May 7, 1887 edition purports to print letters to *Punch* from distinguished personages, including Gladstone, Henry Irving and Buffalo Bill, signed by very ungenuine signatures which the paper believes would have been denied by the persons named. The last was written in an amusing vein, probably more so than Bill Cody himself could have done. It runs as follows:

My Dear Sir,

You evidently, in common with the rest of the British Public, have fallen into the trap artfully laid for you by the coloured posters, and are associating my advent in this country with the forthcoming performances of the *Wild West Show* about to be held at the American Exhibition shortly to be opened at Earl's Court. Please dispel the idea from your mind, for my mission over here, which is a double one, is of a very different sort. In the first place I am the accredited agent of the Government of the United States to settle the Fisheries Dispute with the British Cabinet. In the second, I am the first living representative of the part of *Mephistopheles* in my country, and I have come over here to show your Henry Irving how he ought to do it. My reputed connection with the Indians and Cowboys at Earl's Court, you may, therefore, regard as the wildest *canard*. — Yours faithfully,

BUFFALO BILL

From Mr. Alan G. Agnew, Managing Director of *Punch*, comes an explanation of their "Robert" who called himself "the City waiter," whose real name was John T. Bedford. His duty was described by his superior in this way: "If any fun is to be found in the City, I expect you to bring it to me." "Robert" is said to have replied that there "was some to be got out of a City waiter, as waiters were not quite so deaf as was generally considered," a fact often forgotten. A few transcripts are copied from "Robert's" report of his ideas derived from a visit to the Wild West Show:

I never saw such a site as Bufferlow Bill's Wild West in South Kensington, the werry reklekshun of it sets me off so that I must pull myself together with one of Bertram's "Brighton Steadiers," or I shall get too exsited to write strait.

Well, I spose it was because they was jest a little late that the whole blooming lot of 'em, Amerrycans and Cow Boys, and Mexicans and Injians with their Squalls and Porposes, and Gals a riding like gals generally rides, and Gals a riding like men, all cum a galloping in at such a whirling pace that it litorally took away all my pore breth, and they screamed as they galloped, and their crimson and blue and scarlet and yeller clokes all shone in the sunlight and fluttered in the breeze, and when they came jest in front of me, where I was setting with dignerty in a reserwed seat at the small charge of 1s., they pulled up bang, as if they was all shot and all sat as still as mice.

Well, then we had a hole carrywan of settlers for life attacked as they was agoing quietly along by a hole army of wild Injians, and defended by Bufferlow Bill and his bold Cow Boys, and a grand fight it was. Plenty of firing, but not enuff execushun for to friten the ladies, for tho jest a few was killed in the dedly combat, they all got up and rode away after the battle was over; so I spose as they was ony shamming jest to deceeve the enemy.

Curiosity, which is the Waiter's weekness, makes me inquire, why so many Cow Boys when there aint not no Cows? We wound up with a Bufferlow hunt, but as the animals was jest as uncurrycombed and as dirty as afore, I gammoned Mrs. Robert, who was with me, that it was ardly a site for a reel dellycat lady to witness. . .

Hoping to meet with the Kernel who had promised to introduce me to the Hon. Mr. William Bufferlow, Esquire, wulgerly called Bufferlow Bill, I sauntered round to the Injians encampment, but was there told he had gone to dine with some other Savages at the Savage Club (actual name of a London club) so I couldn't see him.

. . . But I have sum dim recklekshun of playing at cards with two Chiefs and a Squaw, and that one of

THE BUFFALO BILLERIES.
By Dumb Crambo Junior.

The Wild *West* Show.

Boss and "Bos."

King of the Cowboys and Duke of Bucking 'em.

See-you Chief combing his Wig-wam.

A Lass-o with a Lasso.

Squaws and Squawls.

Injin-earring Department.

Our Artist is persuaded to try a mount. When last seen he was still soaring toward the setting sun.

THE BUFFALO BILLERIES
Reproduced by permission of PUNCH, *Alan S. Agnew, Managing Director*

them had a dress on sumthink like a porkypine with his squills, and that I lost my money, and that sum familyer voice said, "Why, Robert, you've lost your Injian Rubber!" at witch we all larfed.

There is a picture of Robert playing an "Indian Rubber" with an Indian Chief.

A few of the verses written by *Punch* go with the picture of —

WILD WEST-MINSTER!

Air — "Do you ken John Peel?"

Do you ken Arthur Peel in the nightly fray?
Do you ken Arthur Peel, at the break of day?
Do you think he won't wish himself far far away,
    Ere the House rises early in the morning?

Chorus.

For the sound of the Pats keeps us each from our bed,
And the Tory horse bolts if you give him his head,
And the row of the Rads, by sly LABOUCHERE led,
    At Wild West-minster sounds until morning.

Yes, I know Arthur Peel, with his seat so true,
And he needs it indeed on that buck-jumping screw,
Which to fling Arthur Peel has done all that it knew,
    The bit and the bridle still scorning.

Do you ken Arthur Peel of the resolute will,
And the "hand" that is worthy of Buffalo Bill?
Do you think the buck-jumper would not like to spill
    The cool hand on its back ere the morning?

Yes, I know Arthur Peel for a rough-riding body,
At handling a rogue almost equal to Cody,
And down like a hammer on noodle and noddy,
    Though kept in the saddle till morning.

. . .

PUNCH, OR THE LONDON CHARIVARI.—May 14, 1887.

WILD WEST-MINSTER!

OR, "BUCK-JUMPING" EXTRAORDINARY!!

Reproduced by permission of PUNCH, Alan S. Agnew, Managing Director

We are informed by Mr. Agnew that the rider of the bucking bronco was supposed to be Arthur Wellesley Peel (Viscount Peel), Speaker of the House of Commons 1884-1895. Drawn by George du Maurier.

Do you ken Arthur Peel with the spur at his heel,
Which the stubbornest buck-jumper's bound for to feel,
And flinch at the punishment dealt out by Peel,
　　While Wild West-minster howls in the morning?

　　　　　　　.　　.　　.

Chorus.

For the sound of its snorts and the pad of its feet
Show this buck-jumping brute is a teaser to beat,
And Peel will do well if he still keeps his seat
　　When Wild West-minster shuts some fine morning.

DEDHAM TAVERNS AND STAGECOACHES

DEDHAM WAS ONE of the important stagecoach centers as it was on the direct route from Boston to New York, via Hartford. As a memento of that era the town of Westwood, just south of Dedham, still has a long street named Hartford, over which the stages passed. It was quite natural, therefore, that quite a few inns should spring up which have been so well described by the late Walter Austin in his *Tale of a Dedham Tavern.* The Norfolk House, known also as the Norfolk Hotel, became in 1910 the property of Austin as his private residence, and as it is situated in Court Street, it was on the direct stage road, extending at one time from Portsmouth, New Hampshire, through Boston, Dedham, Providence, New York and as far south even as James City, Virginia. The Norfolk House for a number of years was the most active of those in Dedham, so much so that a writer in the *Dedham Transcript* on March 6, 1909, remarked that, in 1832, sixteen hundred stages went in and out of Boston weekly and that thirty coaches left early every morning on their long journey from Boston to New York, adding the impolite remark which would be disputed by musicians and others, that "taverns were as thick as fiddlers in hell." This Inn was also on the route of the Norfolk and Bristol Turnpike, called the Lower Road, which in 1804 ran through Dedham, Westwood and Islington from Boston to New Haven and New York. The particularly interesting diary of the prominent Nathaniel Ames, Jr. of Dedham, records the stages as starting from Boston at 4:00 A.M., passing by the tavern, then known as Marsh's, and reaching Hartford at 8:00 P.M., adding that it "runs it in 16 hours, 100 m. — little more than 6 m. an hour without stop — but relays every 10 miles." This gives an idea of the number of horses necessary for this comparatively short run.

From "Tale of a Dedham Tavern" by Walter Austin
Courtesy of Mrs. Walter Austin

THE ORIGINAL ALDEN'S TAVERN, DEDHAM, MASSACHUSETTS

known also at various times by the name Norfolk House or Norfolk Hotel, and by other names. Although much changed it is now owned and occupied by Mrs. Walter Austin. It was situated on Court Street and still stands on its original site.

The year 1795 seems to have brought about great advances in stagecoaching, road building, travel and mails and at one period it was a question as to which of three routes from Boston to Hartford shown on the map would be chosen. By a vote of the Legislature in February of 1800, it was decided to use this Mid-post or Middle road through Westwood Center, as it was designated, which passed through Dedham. The Boston to Providence turnpike was approved two years later. "Though some citizens dread it," according to Ames' diary, "as bad as a standing army to spunge them of money." This legislation, of course, greatly pleased the townspeople, especially the tavern keepers. There was apparently some sort of a line, run irregularly, five years previously. Mention of Dedham as a stopping place of this line reminds one of the remark made recently by an enthusiastic Bostonian who said he motored to California by way of Dedham.

Martin Marsh, once owner of the Norfolk House, believed that the acquisition of a stage line would fit in well with his business of landlord, therefore he started one to Boston in 1814. The fare was 62½¢ and his local advertisement read in part, "Neat and convenient carriages, fleet and gentle horses, civil and obliging drivers, will constantly be provided . . . Small bundles carried and errands punctually done for the usual price." This reminds the writer that Whall, the Milton expressman of a later day, used to take orders for the residents of that town and one distinguished lady on Milton hill instructed him to select a new hat for her whenever she thought it necessary to make a change.

In the same newspaper, under "Welcome and Good Cheer!" is mentioned the "Tavern in the brick house adjoining the Court House in Dedham," with "pure Wines" and "good Spirits," adding "Parties of Pleasure are informed that he has a large and convenient Hall for Dancing," which the present generation of Dedhamites have enjoyed up to recently. In 1828 one of the many owners of the Tavern advertised that arrangements had been made to have relays of horses at his "House" which cannot help recalling the days when at the Polo Club on High Street very often were stabled as many as sixty polo ponies which could be seen being exercised along the town streets. Times certainly have changed. Another stage line went to Boston three times a week by "the several manufacturing establishments in Dedham; and thence to the Brush Hill Turnpike, direct to Boston." (Seems very indirect.) A few years later landlord Francis Alden advertises, showing a cut of the tavern, for "a few *genteel boarders* from the city or country."

Worthington's *History of Dedham*, published in 1827, contains a paragraph referring to the arrival of the stages:

Every other day the mail arrives on its way to Washington City. The number of those who assemble at the Post Office at the hour of arrival is not so great that each one must ask a question and be off, but custom allows the talkers and the quid nuncs to remain, and amuse or oppress their temporary audience with their remarks on all subject.

Naturally there was intense rivalry between stagecoaches. especially from Boston to Providence, and each line of course had its favorite stopping place. The Peoples' Line changed horses at the Norfolk Hotel and the rival Citizens' Line made a halt at the nearby Phoenix House on the corner of High and Washington Streets, well named as both buildings and stables were burned twice, destroying many horses each time. For a while, between fires, it was a very popular resort. Referring again to the keen competition, a contributor to the *Dedham Transcript* wrote:

One of the excitements to arouse the town out of its lethargy was the arrival of the stage coaches at Bride's (Phoenix) or Alden's

From an old painting in the Dedham Historical Society
Courtesy of Miss Elizabeth R. Humphreys

THE OLD PHOENIX HOTEL, OR BRIDE'S TAVERN, DEDHAM

Corner of High and Washington Streets, which burned in 1832. A later building burned in 1880. This is the only picture known to us.

(Norfolk House) tavern on their way from Providence to Boston. Then for a few moments all was hurry and bustle, the stage horn would be heard in the distance, and the horses would be brought to the door all harnessed and ready, and in less time than I could tell it the tired horses are taken out and fresh ones put in and the stage is on its way, the Citizens' and the Peoples' Line striving to see which shall make the shortest time.

The *Providence Gazette* had an amusing description of this journey:

> We were rattled from Providence to Boston in 4 hours and 50 minutes, and if any one wants to go faster, he may send to Kentucky and charter a streak of lightening.

As to the speed in changing horses, the *Norfolk Advertiser* bragged that the Dedham hostlers made it "handsomely in one minute." That there were accidents in those days is apparent from a local newspaper, which reported that two chaises collided in front of the Norfolk Inn, knocking down a pillar of the portico.

Dancing was fully as much in vogue in the early days as now and many parties came from Boston, Quincy and other towns in Norfolk County to test the ball room at the Norfolk House, which many of the recent generations have enjoyed equally much. An article in the *Dedham Transcript*, by E. W. Virgin, states: "From far and near parties of quality came to try the celebrated spring floor and the elegant game suppers following a royal dance." This attractive room forms a part of this beautiful tavern, — residence now of Mrs. Walter Austin. To those of the writer's generation the only spring floor that could compete with this Dedham one belonged to the noted dancing teacher Papanti, who held classes for many years on Tremont Street in Boston. Of this Norfolk ball room the *Dedham Transcript* has a good deal to say —

> . . . as it yielded to the even step of the merry dancers it would rise and fall like the waves upon a gentle sea; at the same time the doors and windows in the second story beneath would rattle as if buffeted by a storm . . . The square dance was then all the go; the round dance as yet had not caught in its fond embrace the Dedham lad and bonny lassie.

NORFOLK HOTEL.

From "Tale of a Dedham Tavern" by Walter Austin
Courtesy of Mrs. Walter Austin

THE TAVERN, IN 1829

This inn, much changed, is shown in two other pictures. It is
owned and occupied by Mrs. Walter Austin.

This widely-known floor had to be resurfaced and it is
regretted that the spring was removed. The present owner very
proudly showed the writer over her many-roomed attractive
house. Here in her sitting room, she explained, used to be the
bar. The eye, however, could not help noticing the unique and
beautiful staircase, exceeded in quaintness and originality only
by the famous stairway in the Knox Mansion at Thomaston,
Maine. The Dedham one has four ways of entrance, going in a
two-way staircase to the second story, and from there a two-way
stairway extends up still another story. One realizes how many
travelers could find accommodation here. The dances indulged
in are indicated in an advertisement by a teacher in 1837. It
reads: "Mr. A. Deuchar . . . will teach Waltzes, Gallopades and
Mazourkas, which have become so very popular and fashionable.

Particular attention will be given to instruction in *attitudes*. It was the day of the "contra-dance," — the first gentleman "to foot it to the second lady and both turn single," — "first three couples haze," — "three hands round with the second lady," etc., now coming into favor again at country clubs and elsewhere.

A well known teacher of this "polite accomplishment" was Lovet Stimson, (not an ancestor of the distinguished lawyer, diplomat and author, Frederic J. Stimson,) who "respectfully informs the inhabitants of Dedham that his school for the instruction of young Masters and Misses in the polite accomplishments of Dancing will commence . . . at Mr. Gragg's Hall." (Another name for the Norfolk Tavern.) Later he will also teach "Cotillions" . . . "the most fashionable dances." A good many

From "Tale of a Dedham Tavern" by Walter Austin
Courtesy of Mrs. Walter Austin

THE NORFOLK HOUSE, OR NORFOLK HOTEL, AS IT APPEARS TODAY

The ball room, once so popular, is at the back of the house.
Dedham had many taverns as it was on the direct road from
Boston to Providence and New York.

years later he added to his list the Polka, Schottische, Redo-
way and Brilliants, and if any of his pupils could master this
variety of steps how popular they must have been!

A Thanksgiving ball was held at Capt. Alden's Hall (the
Norfolk) in the winter of 1836, and at that time the popularity
of the dance induced these few lines:

> Come fix up your ruffles, your ribbons and lace,
> Let dimples and ringlets now deck every face,
> Bring plumes, wreaths and roses, gems, diamonds and all,
> And prepare to attend the grand Thanksgiving Ball.

The Phoenix shared some of the success achieved by the
Norfolk and at one time it was one of the finest in the country.
Here took place during the winter months several "Social
Assemblies" at which, according to an editorial in the *Norfolk
Democrat* in 1841, "the music is of the tallest kind; those who
have not heard it had better brush up their pumps and test its
merits." This tavern was known as the Temperance House and
attracted for a time a certain class of customers. At a Fireman's
Muster in the year 1851 many of the companies had their headquarters there and one of the toasts, which under the rules must
have been drunk in water, was to the "Ladies, — encouraged
by their smiles, the fireman fears no foe; and can only be subdued
when combatting fires of their own kindling."

A story is told of Woodward's Tavern, which stood near
High Street, on the corner of Court Street. The proprietor,
Richard by name, must have been quite romantic for he cut
heart-shaped openings in the shutters of the tap room, and in
the evenings when the light showed through these openings,
passers-by often remarked: "See the light shine through Mrs.
Woodward's heart." This tavern in 1649 was licensed to
Joshua Fisher, a name well known in the town's history. In
this tavern is mentioned the "Great Room" where not only
travelers by land but workmen who rowed lumber up and
down the Charles River were wont to quench their thirst. The

From a sketch in the Dedham Historical Society
Courtesy of Miss Elizabeth R. Humphreys

THE OLD FISHER-AMES-WOODWARD TAVERN
One of the Earliest Inns in Dedham

This old tavern dates back to 1658, but is no longer standing. It was owned by Joshua Fisher from 1658 to 1730; by Nathaniel Ames, Sr. from 1735 to 1766 and by Richard Woodward during the Revolution. It was taken down in 1817. It stood near High Street on the easterly side of the road from the "Keye" on Charles River. It was on this building that Ames hung his caricature signboard, described in another chapter.

rivers in that day were one of the principal highways for industry. In this so called "Great Room" similar to those which existed also in other inns, there was often a box attached to the wall where donations might be left for the servants of the house. This was usually marked T I P, short for "To insure promptness," It has been said that from these letters originated the word "Tip."

Some years later, in 1735, Dr. Nathaniel Ames, Senior, through his marriage, became landlord. He is known as "the celebrated almanack maker," for he published thirty-eight annuals, the first one in 1725 when he was only sixteen years of age. His predictions were so very accurate that he once re-marked that "people required more information of an almanack maker, about future events, than was known by the devil." Sam¹ Briggs printed these almanacks which ran from 1726 to 1775 and a few of his remarks are inserted here. Nathaniel Ames "a physician, and inn-keeper of Dedham, a man of original, vigorous and pungent genius began the publication of his Astro-nomical Diary and Almanack." A commentator said that "from the first, it contained in high perfection every type of excellence afterwards illustrated in the almanac of Benjamin Franklin. Indeed, according to Briggs, Ames' Almanack was in most respects, better than Franklin's, adding that "He freely predicted future events, but always with a merry twinkle in his eye . . . extremely readable and sure to raise shouts of laughter around thousands of fireplaces where food for laughter was much needed." These remarks have been included as Ames, the Senior, was such a talented man in so many different ways. Roger Sherman of Connecticut, and a signer of the Declaration of Independence, started an almanac, referring at the same time to "the ingenious and celebrated Dr. Ames, with whom you are well acquainted. Still another compliment was paid to the Senior Ames by the editor of the almanack. "If there ever was anything in Ames' Almanack, which more than another caused my heart to go out to that enterprising New England Astron-omer-Physician, it was the knowledge of the fact that he was an inn-keeper, who fully appreciated the importance of his calling, and hesitated not to own the "sorry trade," yet withal, to caution the guest against the serpent that lurked within the bowl. Still another connoisseur of almanacs claimed that Ames's were superior to those of his contemporaries and had a large circula-tion of about 60,000 copies throughout New England; he also stated that they nearly superseded all others. Many were printed on paper made in Milton. Ames had his eye, evidently, on the business side of his undertakings for he printed this advertisement in at least one issue of his almanack in 1751:

These are to signify to all Persons that travel the great Post-Road South-West from Boston, that I keep a House of Publik Entertainment Eleven Miles from Boston, at the Sign of the Sun. If they want Refreshment, and see Cause to be my Guests, they shall be well entertained at a Reasonable Rate. N. Ames.

The writer of the book, Dr. Ames, Senior, in a note calls it a new business departure, and boldly announces himself as a tavern keeper. These almanacks doubtless brought a good deal of trade to his inn. In 1763 Dr. Ames also inserted a request that Innkeepers keep him posted as to new License owners, distances of their Inns from stages, list of post roads, and acceptable houses of entertainment. Upon his death in 1764 his widow kept the Tavern and after her marriage to Richard Woodward the Inn was known as The Woodward Tavern, as mentioned previously.

Landlords were not always mild tempered for Woodward got into an altercation with the younger Ames. "Old Woodward struck me with his saw," he wrote. He was fined by the court, but said he would "fleece his estate as much as possible," which he did a few months later by carrying off some loads of rye, corn and hay.

Not every traveler got pleasure at an inn, as shown by a visitor, with a French name, who, some years later, according to Samuel Briggs, came to Dedham and stated, "I had read so much," he wrote, "about the quaint old town, that I had mentally erected, and soon came to believe that I should find there the veritable old Tavern in which the Almanacks were written; where 'Physick' was dispensed, where the jovial, hearty, grand old landlord had 'welcomed the coming, sped the parting guest.' A hostelry, where the mail coach in His Majesty's service had regularly stopped, where the horses were changed, and passengers either alighted for a stay, or to step in for a 'drop of something comforting.' Exchanging pleasant greetings the while with the host, and granting a smile for a 'curtsey' to the plumpest and cheeriest of barmaids. But, alas! I didn't find it — nor even a substitute for it. But I did find an Historical Society, and as genial and enthusiastic a gathering of antiquarian students as one could ever desire to meet."

A son, named for the father, continued the Almanack for about ten years, now a rare relic in the Dedham Historical Society, and also wrote his own instructive diary, quoted in this chapter, from 1758 to 1821. He commenced this work while in College, and one entry mentioned that he helped the President by raking the hay in his front field. This unusual Doctor lived in small-pox days and the number of "jabs" made during eleven years by Dr. Stimson, Dr. Thayer, Dr. Wheaton and himself was recorded in the so-called "Vaccination Book," in which also Frederic Stimson and others entered the early history of the Dedham Polo Club. This book is now in the collection of the Historical Society.

Many events took place in the Dedham taverns. One of the many toasts on one occasion was to "The Female Sex — The best and handsomest piece of domestic furniture is a virtuous, and amiable woman."

Many sleighing parties stopped at one of the Dedham inns for "refreshments" and to warm up for the drive home, and at one time, probably on a very cold night, a resident remarked that his "house" (Inn) was the new place for the sleigh-riders — and the way the mulled wine was disposed of was a caution." In 1822 a "learned" elephant proved a great attraction at the Norfolk Inn, and a poster of this "Sagacious and Docile" animal must have excited the curiosity of many visitors at the low price of 12½¢ per person. In the ball room once took place a concert by the Ethiopian Serenaders which was well attended. A very full meeting of lovers of "Sweet sound" was held one evening at Alden's (Norfolk Inn), according to a diary, with the admonition "to eat, drink and sing with moderation, temperance and perfection — and each one be at liberty to *license himself*." There were also many Masonic meetings, as well as the annual dinners of the novel Society for Apprehending Horse

Thieves, causing the present generation of horse owners to refer jokingly to it as the "Organization for the Apprehension of Cruelty to Horse Thieves."

The Norfolk Mutual Fire Insurance Company, now the successful Norfolk and Dedham Fire Insurance Company, was organized at the Norfolk Inn in 1825, with John Endicott as President.

The Boston and Providence Railroad extension to Dedham in 1834 — two trips each day — about the same as today! — put an end to the stagecoach days. As Walter Austin said in the *Tale of a Dedham Tavern*, already referred to in this chapter, "Vale the Stage-coach!"

The stages occasionally by-passed Dedham and continued several miles southward to the Ellis Tavern in West Dedham, now Westwood, on the Middle Road, and from the Farmer's Almanac for the year 1795, Ernest J. Baker, so well posted on the history of this locality, points out that on the "Road to Newport" this inn is listed as a stagecoach station. The Ellis family has a unique place in Westwood's history. Three brothers came to Dedham as early as 1642; two removed elsewhere, but Richard settled here and the seven generations of his family, as Ernest Baker describes it, were the "chief concern, delight and admiration" at the one hundredth anniversary of the West Dedham Post Office held in 1924. Of course a descendant of Richard, Abner by name, was chosen first postmaster and the post office was located in the old tavern. (The post office is now in a nearby building.) Although a fire destroyed most of it in 1887, nevertheless there was a small part left, enough to enable the present owners, still the Ellis family, to place on the sign "Ellis Tavern, 1731," and here almost everything can be purchased.

The tavern was not very sizeable as it contained only one room on the lower floor and one chamber.

A lively horse on the signboard of that day would seem to have anticipated the coming of the hunter and the polo pony to this locality a good many years later.

Dr. A. M. Worthington recently added these notes:

The busy time of day was when the stage-coaches arrived. From 12 to 14 came from Boston every morning, sometimes 5 or 6 before breakfast. They were of many colors, always resplendent and business like. The coaches of the Citizen's Line were made in Dedham in the long buildings now used as tenements on Washington Street opposite Williams Street and here some of the finest coaches in the country were turned out. The occupants of the stage-coaches were always interesting to the natives, many coming from distant parts.

From Dedham, and occasionally Westwood, the Middle Road led through the neighboring town of Medfield where stops were often made at Clark's Tavern.

A CARICATURE TAVERN SIGNBOARD

THE WELL KNOWN Ames family of Dedham figured prominently in a number of enterprises described under the chapter on Dedham Inns. Dr. Nathaniel Ames, Sr. who has to do with this particular one, married the daughter of Captain Joshua Fisher in 1735. In this way he inherited the so-called Fisher Inn owned first by Fisher, Sr. and then by his son. He became well known as an inn keeper, but not contented with this sole pursuit he spent a greater part of his life writing the remarkable *Ames Almanack* familiar to many New Englanders and others. The site of this Ames Tavern was on the "Road to Connecticut," now High Street, and on the easterly side of the old road from the "Keye" on Charles River, now Washington Street.

The story of Ames' hard-fought legal battle began after the death of his wife's mother and infant child, the details of which would interest lawyers more than our general readers. Dr. Ames brought suit against his wife's family for the ownership of the land and of the Inn itself. The turning point, as stated by Alice Morse Earle in her book *Stage Coach and Tavern Days*, hung upon the decision as to who was the "next of kin."

This prominent Dedhamite was twice defeated in the courts, but nevertheless carried on his petition rigorously in the year 1748 before the Superior Court of the Province of Massachusetts Bay, preparing the case and the argument himself. Finally he achieved success resulting in his getting a decision in his favor, thereby being enabled to change the name of the hostelry from Fisher Inn to Ames Tavern.

Vexed at what he considered undue delay in handing out the verdict, Ames decided to caricature the court which sat on the case. He accordingly set to work to engage an artist to paint a signboard that expressed his opinion of the members of the bench at that time. The author of "The Almanacks of Nathaniel

THE TAVERN SIGN.
From the original sketch found among the papers of Dr. Ames.

Photographed by George M. Cushing, Jr.
Courtesy of Miss Elizabeth R. Humphreys

CARICATURE DEDHAM SIGNBOARD

Placed on Ames Tavern, Dedham, Massachusetts by Dr. Nathaniel Ames, Sr., expressing his disgust at the delay in rendering a legal decision in a lawsuit brought by him. The two judges with their backs turned dissented in the final verdict in Ames' favor.

Ames 1736-1775," Sam[l]. Briggs, printed an illustration of this sign of which there are a few copies in the Dedham Historical Society. One, furnished by Miss Elizabeth R. Humphreys, is reproduced here. On Dr. Ames' original appears this wording which relates to the order given by the tavern owner to the artist for carrying out this work:

Sir: — I wish I could have some talk on ye above subject, being the bearer waits for an answer shal only observe Mr. Greenwood thinks ye can not be done under £40 Old Tenor.

The pleasure Dr. Ames had in seeing the signboard set up must have fully compensated him for the sum expended.

This reproduction requires an explanation: Two of the judges, Chief Justice Paul Dudley and Benjamin Lynde, dissented in the verdict and therefore Dr. Ames featured these two on the sign with their backs turned. The others are supposed to be rather good likenesses of the other judges. The open book in front of them represents the "Province Laws." Over the head of the Chief Justice, the center figure, are shown the arms of Great Britain, and above is the inscription *Nearest a Kin to Fisher*. The others on the caricature tavern signboard are Richard Saltonstall, Samuel Sewall, once Chief Justice and John Cushing. The rest cannot be identified. We are glad to notice that the ancestor of our Senator Leverett Saltonstall does not have his back turned.

The Court was informed of this insulting signboard and decided to send a messenger to Dedham to remove it. As chance would have it, Ames happened to be in Boston at that same time, got advance information and was determined to get home first. He must have had a speedy horse, or else pushed him faster, for he reached his tavern in time to remove his scurrilous painting. He was just able to replace the sign with another, done very hurriedly, to welcome the sheriff when he arrived, on which this inelegant wording appeared: "A Wicked and adulterous generation seeketh after a sign, and there shall no sign be given unto it."

A copy of the new sign never made its way to the Dedham Historical Society, yet the old tavern, perhaps due somewhat to the publicity of this episode, became more prosperous even than before. It is a pity that neither of these odd signs was preserved, but doubtless the owner believed it would be wiser to destroy them lest some high authority might search the premises. Nevertheless, many Dedhamites must have had a good laugh over the incident.

SIGNBOARD HUMOR

Samuel A. Drake and Walter K. Watkins in their book on "Old Boston Taverns" mention a curious sign not, however, complimentary to the gentler sex. It showed the figure of a female without a head and was hung outside an inn known as "Good Woman" in the North End of Boston. It is said this sign did not remain long. Other similar signs were inscribed "Quiet Woman" and "Silent Woman." These authors speak of a signboard showing a bird, a tree, a ship and a can, with this amusing legend:

> This is the bird that never flew,
> This is the tree which never grew,
> This is the ship which never sails,
> This is the can which never fails.

Also mentioned is an inn with a special appeal to the sailor, the inscription on the signboard being worded:

> With sorrows I am compass'd round,
> Pray lend a hand, my ship's aground.

Another nautical couplet composed to attract the seafarer is:

> Coil up your ropes and anchor here
> Till better weather doth appear.

One stanza refers to refreshments that could be obtained at a certain tavern:

> What d'you think
> Here's a good drink
> Perhaps you may not know it.
> If not in haste, stop in and taste
> You merry folks will show it.

Another "drink" sign mentioned by Alice Morse Earle in her *Stage Coach and Tavern Days* has this lettering:

> Rove not from sign to sign, but stop in here,
> Where naught exceeds the prospect but the beer.

This sign inscription is rather amusing:

> Pause traveler here,
> Just stop and think
> A weary man
> Must need a drink.

A signboard in London bore this lettering:

> I, William McDermott lives here,
> I sells good porter, ale and beer,
> I've made my sign 'a little wider
> To let you know I sell good cider.

The signs in this country were not quite as varied as the incongruous combinations which we are told existed in England some years ago. A student of the subject mentions these examples:

> I'm amazed at the signs
> As I pass through the town,
> To see the odd mixture,
> A Magpie and Crown,
> The Whale and the Crow,
> The Razor and Seven stars,
> The Axe and the Bottle,
> The Tun and the Lute,
> The Eagle and Child,
> The Shovel and Boot.

Edward Field in *The Colonial Tavern* writes of a sign on each side of which was a rhyme concerning the highway nearby:

> Before you do this hill go up,
> Stop and drink a cheering cup.

On the reverse appeared:

> You're down the hill all danger's past,
> Stop and drink a cheerful glass.

A comforting signboard in Rhode Island read:

> Whate'er may tend to soothe the soul below,
> To dry the tear and blunt the shaft of woe,
> To drown the ills that discompose the mind,
> All those who drink at Warwick's Inn shall find.

A Salem tavernkeeper, named Symonds, placed on his sign-board this verse:

> Francis Symonds Makes and Sells
> The best of Chocolate, also Shells,
> I'll toll you if you have need,
> And feed you well, and bid you speed.

There is another story of a curious sign told by Mary Caroline Crawford. At a tavern on the Neck near the Roxbury line was a sign showing a globe with a man breaking through the circumference very much like a chicken coming out of the shell. The motto read: "Oh, how shall I get through this world?" An onlooker, rather shabbily clad, replied to the motto to the amusement of the others, "List, and you'll get through this world fast enough."

The most curious and amusing signboard was a caricature painted for one of Dedham's most learned and prominent citizens. Dr. Nathaniel Ames, Sr., physician, "almanack" maker and tavern keeper, as told in a previous chapter.

Of course the signs afforded much fun for boys who occasionally painted them over or even ran away with them, leaving something amusing to replace them.

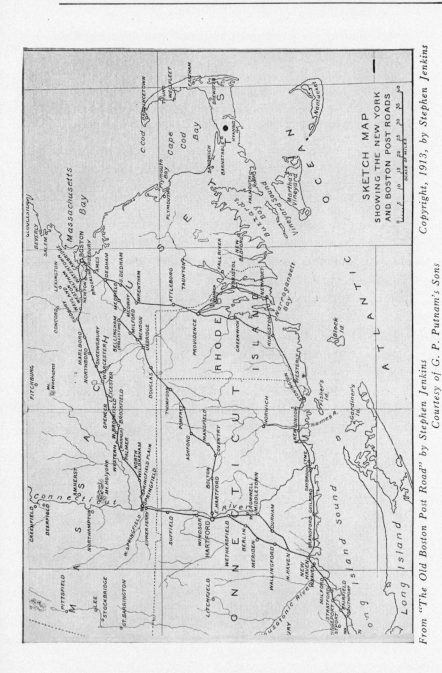

SKETCH MAP

SHOWING THE NEW YORK
AND BOSTON POST ROADS

From "The Old Boston Post Road" by Stephen Jenkins

Courtesy of G. P. Putnam's Sons

Copyright, 1913, by Stephen Jenkins

MAP SHOWING THE MOST IMPORTANT STAGECOACH LINES OUT OF BOSTON

KNIGHTS OF THE WHIP

THE NEW HAMPSHIRE HISTORICAL SOCIETY has a clipping entitled "A Glorification of Stage-Drivers" which runs as follows:

> . . . there is magic in the calling of a stage driver. Everybody knows and aspires to know the stage-driver; everybody is known by, and is proud to be known by the stage-driver. The little boys remember it a month, if the stage-driver speaks to them. There is a particular satisfaction to be able to distinguish among drivers and say it was Winkle, or it was Hines, or it was Mitchell. Of all the people on the earth, he is the one who rolls by in a gilded coach; he is the one who sweeps it high and dry over the world; he is the one who rides through his immense estate with the most lordly and consequential air, and all the rest of us seem to be but poor tenants and gaping boors. It is something to speak to a stage-driver; it is a great thing to be able to joke with him.

> It is a sign of a great man to be recognized by the stage-driver. To be, perchance, known by one who knows nobody is nothing; to be known, to be pointed out, to have your name whispered in a bystander's ear by one who knows everybody, affects you as if Omniscience were speaking about you. The stage-driver differs from a steamboat captain in that the latter is not seen to be so immediately connected with his craft as the former . . . How the villagers — the blacksmith, the shoemaker, the thoughtful politician, and the boozy loafers that fill the stoop — grin and stare and make their criticisms!

> How he flings the reins and the tired horses to the stable-boy, who presently returns with a splendid relay! How he accepts these from the boy, with that sort of air with which a king might be supposed to take his crown from the hands of a valet! There are his gloves, withal; he always wears gloves, as much as a Saratoga fine lady, and would no sooner touch anything without gloves, than such a lady would a glass of Congress water.

Stage drivers were indeed a class by themselves; they were almost invariably capable, possessed of great endurance and, accustomed to hardships, were resourceful, honest, skilful in their way, almost always polite and accommodating. Their life was indeed a rugged one.

Walter Austin in his *Tale of a Dedham Tavern*, owned by him, has reproduced an article written by Samuel McIntire in an issue of the *Dedham Transcript* in 1902:

> Reverting again to my boyhood, those were the good old days of the stage coach, and often as I stood upon the rustic porch of the old Norfolk House, have watched with the keenest interest the driver perched upon his high seat, circle his four in hand at full speed, around and up in front of the porch, with the precision of a master. It was done so nicely and with such ease that I wished I was old enough to be in the driver's place; indeed I thought at the time that the driver of a stage coach was about as exalted a position as a person could well occupy, and the sharp crack of the whip as the driver swung the long lash to bring the leaders into place was music in my ears and made me long to handle that whip and try its snapping qualities.

There are more than the usual number of stories attached to stage drivers and most of them seem to place this special class of men on a high pinnacle of esteem and importance. Several writers on this subject tell of a driver who evidently considered himself at the top of his profession. This individual from Salem is reported to have angrily answered a hungry passenger who kept urging him to drive faster — "Don't tell me what to do; when I drive this coach I am the whole United States of America."

They seemed to enjoy their pursuit, judging from the statement repeated by Frederick A. Currier in the Fitchburg Historical Society to the effect that the hardest days of the week were the Sundays, "when he missed the old swaying motion of the coach, which was to him as soothing as the rocking of a cradle to an infant." One driver is said to have covered 135,000 miles in his day. An example of fondness for this trade was a citizen of Athol who decided to give up stage driving with its many hardships and to retire to a life of ease. Mrs. Earle in her story of stages tells the rest of the tale:

On the third day of his life on the farm he stood at the edge of a field as a stage passed on the road. The driver gave "the Happy Farmer" a salute and snapped his whip. The horses started ahead on the gallop, a passenger on top waved good-by to him; the coach bounded on and disappeared. Farmer Bryant walked sombrely across the field to his new home, packed his old carpet-bag, went to the stage-office in the next town, and two days later he swept down the same road on the same coach, snapping his whip, waving his hand, leaving the miles behind him. He was thus one week off the coach-box. . . .

We imagine the drivers as huge, burly individuals, but this was not always the case for a writer on coaching speaks of a Groton man named Phin who was so small that on stormy nights he used to put his feet inside one of the lamps so as to keep them warm. The same author (Tristam) told a well known knight of the whip one day that he could whistle louder, hit a horse harder and tell a bigger lie than any one he ever knew.

Another rather stern driver happened to be handling the "ribbons" on a coach which had three classes of fares. Of course most of the passengers chose the low price tickets and for a time on the road they wondered why there was this difference in the price of transportation. Presently they came to the hill and to the surprise of the travelers the second class was ordered to alight and walk, and the third class had to get out and push the stage. Presently they all paid first class fares.

Here is another description of a driver:

What a prince of drivers was Driver Day! Handsome, dressy, and a perfect lady's man! How many ladies were attracted to a seat on the box beside him! How many young men envied his grace as a driver! So, also, what gentlemen were the tavern-keepers of that day! They studied to please the public by their manners. . . .

Hon. Allen W. Dodge expressed well his admiration of the stage drivers, particularly from the point of view of the younger generation:

In those days of old-fashioned winters, there were many trials and difficulties in getting through the route, but let the storm or the snow blockade be ever so bad, they were always ready in their turn to do to the uttermost all that men could do to accomplish it. These drivers, too, were the most obliging and kind-hearted men that ever handled reins, cracked whip or sounded stage horn.

They were great favorites with all the boys who rode with them. Many of us who were then at Exeter Academy came home at the end of the term by the Eastern Stage route, and a lively time we used to have of it. Quite a number of stage coaches were always sent on to take us. When they arrived what a scramble ensued to see who should ride with Pike, who with Annable, or Knight, or Forbes, or some other good-natured driver — experienced in stages and careful of their young charges, as if they were all destined to be governors, or judges, or presidents. We used to consider it the seat of honor on the outside with the driver, there to listen to his stories and to enjoy his company. Many a scrap of practical wisdom did we youngsters thus pick up to turn to good account on the great road of life.

A young girl recalls a journey through Portsmouth and Newburyport. "How well I remember," she wrote in after years, "the kind, smiling face of Robinson, as next morning, whip in hand, he appeared at the parlor door and inquired for the 'little girl' who was to go with him! His hearty 'good morning' and 'all ready, miss,' as I presented myself, are still sounding in my ears. While changing horses at Newburyport I was comfortably seated before a warm fire in the sitting-room. Indeed, I do not know that I could have been more comfortably attended to had I been the daughter of the President. I was the daughter of a poor widow instead, and an utter stranger to the man whose memory I have cherished as one of the pleasant recollections of my childhood."

Once when one of the "Knights of the Whip" died and the family was conveying him to the burial ground, the wife shouted out to go as fast as possible because she knew that was the way her husband always liked to go.

Quite often it is related that stage drivers would blow on their horns the equal number of blasts for which they had passengers in order that the innkeeper should know for how many persons to provide food.

In the bar room of the Eagle Hotel in Concord, New Hampshire where a number of parties were given by the drivers, described elsewhere in this brochure, one of their number told a story recorded in the New Hampshire Historical Society. One of the stable men was rather well known as a petty thief, but in spite of this fault he was so good natured that he was, nevertheless, quite a favorite. One of those who congregated in the hotel suggested that it would be nice to have a chicken supper, whereupon a wager was made by one of the drivers present that John, the hostler, could not provide such a meal. John accepted the proposition and soon appeared with five nice hens. Everyone wondered whose chickens they were and later it was learned that they came from the hen roost of the man who had made the bet.

An unknown author compiled the following verse which takes one back to the days of the driver:

> The road, the road, the turnpike road
> The hard, the brown, the smooth, the broad
> Without a mark, without a bend
> Horses 'gainst horses on it contend.
> Men laugh at the gates, they bilk the tolls
> Or stop and pay like honest souls.
> I'm on the road, I'm on the road;
> I'm never so blithe as when abroad
> With the hills above and the vales below
> And merry whereso'er I go.

FATHER OF THE STAGE
AND THE TURNPIKE

THE SUBJECT of this chapter is Levi Pease, born in Enfield, Connecticut, and later a resident of Boston and then Shrewsbury, who, starting as a blacksmith, established one of the earliest stagecoach lines hereabouts, became one of the important tavern proprietors, received the first government mail contract in 1786, and twenty-two years later obtained the first government charter for a turnpike road in Massachusetts. Added to these achievements he served with unusual distinction throughout the Revolutionary War in very special assignments, including the duties of purchasing agent for the horses necessary to drag the French artillery from Newport, Rhode Island to Yorktown, Virginia.

After the war ended, Pease, in 1783, conceived the idea of forming a line of stages to run between Boston and Hartford. With practically no funds on hand he enlisted the interest of another blacksmith and later stage driver, named Reuben Sykes, (sometimes spelled "Sikes") who was able to give the enterprise further impetus. So with everyone frowning on the undertaking the two men established the line, Pease setting out from this city to Hartford at the same time that his partner started from Hartford to Boston. The time allotted was four days each way. For a while few passengers, if any, took advantage of this service, but neither owner would be discouraged. A Bostonian prophesied that the time might come when such a stage line would pay, but not in their lives. These lumbering waggons from Boston left the Lamb Tavern located on the west side of Washington Street on the site later occupied by the well-known Adams House, passing through Northborough, Shrewsbury, Worcester, Springfield and Brookfield, Massachusetts, to Hartford. (The first stage to Providence also put up at the Lamb Tavern.) It wasn't long, however, before travelers began to appear and the finances improved to such an extent that Pease was enabled to purchase an inn in Boston situated opposite the Common, on Tremont Street, where now is located St. Paul's Cathedral.

The line was soon extended through to New York, and when the first trip, some years later, was made between the two places within twenty-four hours, bells were rung and bonfires blazed along the route.

It was about in 1784, that Talmage Hall was brought into the venture and through him the famous Roger Morris Mansion on Harlem Heights was soon made the New York terminal of the Boston stages, under the name of Calumet Hall. The stables took care of the horses and at this dwelling were entertained passengers arriving from Boston and other places. According to Oliver Holmes' (not the well-known poet) story of the stages, Hall furthermore went to much expense in furnishing the house for the accommodation of "parties from town" who could be "served with Breakfast, Dinners, Suppers, Relishes, Teas, Punch, &c. at ten minutes notice." Pease and Sykes, former blacksmiths and later stage drivers, certainly chose well in procuring this attractive house with its beautiful surroundings.

Several books and pamphlets have been written about this famous mansion, one of the most historic in New York City and now standing as a beautiful example of that period. Since it was a stopping place for stages a résumé of its history may prove of interest. An eccentric, rich, attractive, unscrupulous, designing and pompous woman who cut many capers in New York, Saratoga and Paris once occupied it. No wonder it is said this woman left ghosts behind her, who drummed on the panes of her window. She was formerly Betsy Bowen of Providence, Rhode Island, and in 1804 she married Stephen Jumel, a Frenchman, one of the richest merchants of New York. At that time this attractive house was surrounded by woods, tilled fields, farms and orchards. Today the property finds itself amidst numerous houses and apartments, yet its situation on Harlem Heights overlooking two rivers offers much attraction to the visitor who takes the time to journey as far as 160th Street. This "aristocrat among houses," to use the words of William H. Shelton, author of its history, has passed through many vicissitudes, has had numerous owners, and is associated with many historical and fanciful events. It was built in 1765 by Lieut.-Colonel Roger Morris as a summer home and here George Washington established his headquarters for about five weeks. He used the library as his Council Chamber, and here too he received a small delegation of friendly Indians. This event was later made use of by this stagecoach line which advertised that the octagon room in the Morris house in which these Indians had assembled was "very happily calculated for a turtle party." The career of the Jumels was full of troubles until the husband was killed as the result of an accident.

It was not long, however, before this widow of fifty-nine procured another spouse and this time it was a former Vice-President of the United States, Colonel Aaron Burr, then seventy-eight years of age. The marriage took place in the mansion and was one of the most important events that ever occurred there. This union, however, gave her the opportunity, when attending brilliant parties in Paris, of letting herself be known as "the Vice Queen of America." Her weakness seemed to be postilions and four-in-hand coaches, which recalls a story. Once while visiting Saratoga she started for a drive in such an equipage and a well-known person decided to play an amusing trick. He procured a similar coach, postilions and horses, and followed close behind her. This individual was gotten up as a colored woman, and the horses of his postilions were white, whereas Betsy Jumel's, in contrast, were black. This strange scene is said to have created much amusement on the Saratoga streets.

There is another story of Madame Jumel connected with her mansion, later to become a stage center. A visitor related that the owner placed mirrors around the base board of the council chamber to reflect the graceful sweep of the ladies' gowns, while she herself was seated on a dais.

In 1787 Talmage Hall became involved financially and the Jumel halting place had to be given up for a simple tavern at 49 Cortlandt Street, where the Tammany Society held its first recorded meeting. So many stopped here that it became a stage center during the height of the coaching era. Fraunce's Tavern later became the terminal.

The Jumel property was purchased by the City of New York and is under the supervision of the "Washington Headquarters Association" of the Daughters of the American Revolution.

Evidently the owners of the coach lines were constantly searching for more business for in the *Massachusetts Spy* published at Worcester by the noted printer, Isaiah Thomas, there appeared on October 30, 1783 the following advertisement:

Stage Waggons. The subscribers having furnished themselves with convenient Stage Waggons, propose to set off from Hartford on Monday, the 20th of Oct. inst. at 11 o'clock, and arrive at Levi Pease's, Somers, at night . . . The greatest attention will be paid to passengers, by the publick's humble servants.

Levi Pease

Rueben Sikes, Jun.

To return to this stage line, Alice Morse Earle in her tale of stagecoaches quotes Josiah Quincy, who did not seem to be favorably impressed with Pease's line in the earlier days, for he wrote:

I set out from Boston in the line of stages lately established by an enterprising Yankee, Pease by name, which at that day was considered a method of transportation of wonderful expedition. The journey to New York took up a week. The carriages were old and shackling, and much of the harness made of ropes. One pair of horses carried the stage eighteen miles. We generally reached our resting place for the night, if no accident intervened, at ten o'ciock, and after a frugal supper went to bed with a notice that we should be called at three the next morning, which generally proved to be half-past two. Then, whether it snowed or rained, the traveller must rise and make ready by the help of a horn-lantern and a farthing candle, and proceed on his way over bad roads, sometimes with a driver showing no doubtful symptoms of drunkenness, which good-hearted passengers never fail to improve at every stopping place by urging upon him another glass of toddy. Thus we travelled, eighteen miles a stage, sometimes obliged to get out and help the coachman lift the coach out of a quagmire or rut, and arrived at New York after a week's hard travelling, wondering at the ease as well as expedition of our journey.

In 1786 appeared an advertisement in the *Massachusetts Spy* announcing the extension of this service:

Stages from Portsmouth in New Hampshire, to Savannah in Georgia.

There is now a line of Stages established from New Hampshire to Georgia, which go and return regularly, and carry the several Mails, by order and permission of Congress.

The stages from Boston to Hartford in Connecticut, set out, during the winter season, from the house of Levi Pease, at the Sign of the New York Stage, opposite the Mall, in Boston, every Monday and Thursday morning, precisely at five o'clock.

By the present regulation of the stages, it is certainly the most convenient and expeditious way of travelling that can possibly be had in America, and in order to make it the cheapest, the proprietors of the stages have lowered their price from four pence to three pence a mile with liberty to passengers to carry fourteen pounds baggage.

Pease proved himself so reliable in the eyes of the Government as a stagecoach driver and handler of private mails, bundles, etc. that the Post Office department decided to give him the first U. S. mail contract, and this new service first entered Worcester in January of 1786. *Old Times in Shrewsbury, Massachusetts* by Elizabeth Ward gives us this interesting account of Captain Pease's arrival in that town:

. . . when Captain Pease driving four-in-hand awoke the echoes among the hills with the shrill blast from his horn, announcing the arrival of the stage coach, all was excitement until the cloud of dust disappeared and the echo of the horn died away in the distance . . . How he endured the heat and cold and storms, over the rough and ill-kept roads, and how, when the roads were blocked by heavy snow-drifts so that his horses could not travel, he would fasten on his snowshoes, shoulder the mail-bag and plod with his load over Boston Neck.

About this period of the stagecoach (1788) Brissot de Warville, a well known Frenchman, visited this country and wrote accounts of his various travels. The journey over Pease's stage line from Boston to New York gives us an insight into the methods employed by this driver, speaks of several inns where stops were made and tells us of the country through which they drove and the people the visitor met:

> We set out from Boston at four o'clock in the morning, and passed through the handsome town of Cambridge. The country appears well Cultivated as far as Weston, where we breakfasted; thence we passed to Worcester to dinner . . . The Tavern, where we had a good American dinner, is a charming house of wood, well ornamented; it is kept by Mr. Pease, one of the proprietors of the Boston stage.

De Warville admired him for his activity and industry but thought his horses were "over-done with the length and diffi-culty of the courses. . . ." After a night at Spencer he compares our inns favorably with those in France at that time. After passing through Brookfield and Wilbraham, he wrote:

> A small light carriage, well suspended and drawn by two horses, took place of our heavy waggon. We could not conceive how five of us could fit in this little parisian chariot, and demanded an-other. . . . We were obliged to submit. . . . We travelled like lighten-ing . . . I seemed the whole way to be traveling in one of the alleys of the Palais-royal.

He then describes Springfield as resembling a European town with houses near together. Hartford he considered most agree-able and attractive. Weathersfield, Middletown and New Haven seemed to him to display all their treasures of nature. The French traveller wrote, "You will not go into a tavern without meeting with neatness, decency, and dignity. The service at the taverns he described as excellent. Near Fairfield and Rye he said —

I know not which to admire most in the driver, his intrepidity or dexterity. I cannot conceive how he avoided twenty times dashing the carriage in pieces, and how his horses could retain themselves in descending the stair-cases of rocks. One of these is called Horseneck; a chain of rocks so steep, that if a horse should slip, the carriage must be thrown into a valley two or three hundred feet.

On February 15, 1799 the Post Office Department, as a further compliment, asked Pease to set up a line of stages between Philadelphia and Baltimore to carry the mail. "If you are not much engaged at present," the Postmaster wrote, "I should be glad to have you come and purchase the horses, fix the stands, employ the drivers and in fact set the business in motion." The Postmaster followed this up with a later letter, saying "at no period since I have been in the department has my mail been carried with so much regularity and safety as that between Baltimore and Philadelphia."

The next major event in the career of this energetic individual was his appointment by the Government to lay out a turnpike in 1808 from Boston through South Shrewsbury to Worcester. This was one of the first charters of its kind granted in Massachusetts, and soon led to a network of many others. These charters were to private corporations with power to build roads between specified points and to collect tolls. Boston became the hub from which the turnpikes radiated, like spokes, to all the principal surrounding communities. There were turnpikes to Salem, Newburyport, Concord, Dedham, Neponset and Quincy, etc. in addition to the original one to Worcester mentioned above. The Mill Dam, now Beacon Street, was opened as a toll road in 1821 and was so continued until 1868. These roads were much better built and kept in better repair than other highways so people were willing to pay toll for the privilege of using them. Almost without exception in this vicinity the turnpikes were absolutely straight, veering neither to the right nor to the left. When a hill was on the route the turnpike went straight over it. This "bee-line" policy came from the fact that the charters, in defining the routes, generally required that the roads should be built nearly straight, or as straight as possible. It apparently was not realized in those days that it is sometimes as far, as well as a great deal harder, to go over a hill as it would be to go around its base. On the Salem turnpike a small but very deep pond was encountered. The builders would not go around it so they built a floating bridge over it. With the coming of the turnpikes, it was said that stage travel increased to such an extent that drivers of small vehicles had to be careful not to be run into. Perhaps this traffic growth caused a regulation to be passed that "the Driver be furnished with Horns and Trumpets that they shall be Blown on the approach of the Stage to any Post Office and the places where they Dine, Breakfast, etc., etc. and if any Driver refuses to Comply with this Regulation, he must be dismissed by his Employer."

While on the subject of turnpikes it may be interesting to mention that, just as today the rapid transit lines are apt to find spurious coins or slugs in their token boxes, so in the old days there were some folks who tried to avoid the payment of tolls. They were called "shun-pikers." It seems likely that the word "piker" now quite commonly used, came down from the turn-pike days. Webster gives a definition of a piker as "a niggard in money, effort or the like; a tightwad; a shirker." "Shun piker" has been revived of late years to describe tourists and others who prefer to travel along country byways instead of speeding along the modern toll roads. Incidentally, "turnpike" became a term in this country for toll roads in the early days when the roads were blocked by a pole studded with pikes until the traveler paid the toll, whereupon the pole was turned aside to allow continuance along the road.

In 1810 Pease sold his interest in the stage line to Sykes and retired, having sometime previously disposed of his inn on Tremont Mall. He continued to live in Shrewsbury, where he made his headquarters. Sykes moved to Worcester where he

Courtesy of Hiram Harlow

PEASE TAVERN, SHREWSBURY, MASSACHUSETTS

Owned by the well-known stage driver Levi Pease of Boston and Shrewsbury, who established one of the earliest stagecoach lines hereabouts, and made use of this tavern as a convenient stopping place. The line went from Boston to Hartford and later to New York. This building, situated on the Westboro Road, is somewhat changed but is still in existence.

purchased the Exchange Hotel, one of the greatest stage centers in that town.

Pease lived long enough to see his dream completed. The latter years of his life he is described as spending most of his time around his farm and fishing in its brooks, often accompanied by his granddaughter, Eliza. His life work is well summed up in an obituary that appeared in the *Massachusetts Spy* at the time of his death in February 1824:

His enterprise, as well as perseverance, stands conspicuous in his establishing the stages, . . . Like the attempt of Columbus, to discover a Western Continent, his undertaking was pronounced a visionary and ruinous scheme — yet, like the former, he persevered with zeal unabated, and his exertions, like those of the former, were crowned with success. Often did his friends tell him, the establishment was got up one hundred years too soon, that not short of the expiration of that time, would this country be able to support it. He lived, however, to see more than his expectations realized, and to see his posterity, for such he considered the proprietors of the stages, gather richly, and in great abundance of the harvest he had sown. He was not only emphatically the father of the stages, but of the turnpike roads — the first turnpike road in Massachusetts was of his procuring. Few men in his sphere of life, have rendered the community more essential and lasting advantages, and whose services can claim for them, more than his do for him the title of Public Benefactor.

He never was affluent, and though he had brought up a large family, he had wherewith to live comfortably, till a few of the last years of his life, when, his property being nearly exhausted, his friends contributed to his relief, and though he died poor, he died rich in the affections of all, for he had no enemies.

Always happy, and always making the best of everything, he enjoyed life to the last.

A few paragraphs should be added referring to the Pease Tavern in Shrewsbury, previously known as the Farrar Tavern. Its location was at the junction of the Westborough Road and the old King's Highway. It is recorded that two parallel rows of small holes, one above the other, were cut in one side of the house to enable the drivers and others to scramble up to their bunks in the second story, without awakening the guests.

Although not really part of this chapter, another well-known Shrewsbury character was Luther Goddard, who became skillful in repairing watches for his friends, and it is said that every other Sunday, though not ordained, he preached in the town and after the service collected the watches of the parishioners, took them home, repaired them and returned them to their owners on the next preaching day.

FROM STAGE DRIVER
TO RAILROAD BUILDER

B. P. CHENEY

A SIMILAR RISE to that achieved by Benjamin P. Cheney is an accomplishment not too many men have ever experienced. At the age of ten he started work in his father's blacksmith shop, serving for a time as clerk in a tavern at Francestown, soon becoming expressman and then stage driver, the culmination of the honors which came to him being his election as a Director of the Atchison Railroad. The chief factor in this success was his keen vision in seeing opportunities that offered themselves from time to time in the field of transportation. At the early age of sixteen he graduated to the position of driver of the stage between Nashua and Exeter, New Hampshire, and then between Nashua and Keene, a distance of about fifty miles. He continued on this route every day for five years. He became an efficient horseman and at the same time performed many important duties, including the handling of large sums of money to and from the Boston banks. While this article was being prepared a friend in looking it over made the remark that Cheney certainly did better than some armored cars, which recently suffered large losses of funds in their care.

Members of the Cheney family, of which there are a number living around Boston, told us they were brought up on the story that his baldness was caused by carrying so many important packages in his hat, which was doubtless the practice in those days.

From the *New England Historic and Genealogical Register,* through the kindness of Professor Bancroft H. Brown and Miss Hazel Joslyn, Archivist of Dartmouth College, a few sentences have been copied relative to his handling of moneys —

As a young man he handled the reins so skilfully and treated passengers so politely that he became a popular stage-driver on the route to Boston. His chief success was as travelling banker, conveyor of valuable parcels, particularly those containing money. Here he showed rare fidelity and ability; and won such fame that the united stage companies of the Montreal and Boston lines selected him to reside in Boston and manage their whole business of forwarding money and goods.

Soon he combined several connecting stage lines under the name of United States & Canada Express Co. and as recorded above he was employed as general agent and manager of the whole system. In 1889 the old employees of this organization gave their manager a complimentary dinner at Young's Hotel in Boston, the invitation to which event is shown in a reproduction of an original sent us by the New Hampshire Historical Society. The ten courses and thirty-three choices of foods are not reproduced as they would today make our mouths water. The total cost would probably not be as great as a sirloin steak today.

About the year 1840 Cheney moved to Boston and soon established an express business between here and Montreal under the name of Cheney & Co.'s Express. Other mergers followed until in 1879 the entire system became the American Express Co., of which he was given the positions of Treasurer and Director. Through these different appointments he had developed into one of the leading executives in the business. A descendant living in Boston tells us that this well-known express company presented to his grandfather a silver tea set in recognition of his tracking down and convicting the men who robbed an express car between New York and Chicago. It is now part of the Wells Fargo rare collection in San Francisco.

Especially connected with the subject of this brochure was his interest in the overland mail to San Francisco and Wells, Fargo & Co. Express, both of which companies used so many Concord stagecoaches. In addition to his Atchison interests he was also closely associated with the Northern Pacific Railroad. When the Atchison went into bankruptcy in the panic of 1893 he did not avail himself of advance information and did not sell any Atchison stock.

COMPLIMENTARY + DINNER,

... TO ...

Mr. B. P. CHENEY,

BY HIS OLD EMPLOYEES

· OF THE ··

U. S. & CANADA EXPRESS.

From a picture in the New Hampshire Historical Society
Courtesy of Elmer Munson Hunt

Benjamin Pierce Cheney rose from expressman and stage driver to become Director of the Atchison Railroad. This dinner was given him in 1889 by the employees of the United States and Canada Express Company, of which he was the Manager. He was a transportation expert and was held in great respect in New Hampshire, Boston and elsewhere.

During Cheney's staging career he naturally met a number of distinguished persons and among them was Daniel Webster, with whom he formed a lasting friendship. When the latter died in 1852 Cheney presented to the State of New Hampshire a bronze statue of the great orator, done by Thomas Ball. It is on the Capitol grounds in Concord. At the time of the presentation in June of 1886 the donor in an address expressed his satisfaction at being thus able to realize a long cherished ambition of fitly commemorating "a son of New Hampshire, who as a patriot was unexcelled and as an orator and statesman was without a peer." A record of the entire proceedings at the time of the dedication is printed in a pamphlet now in the New Hampshire Historical Society. A large procession also took place and the exercises were attended by many prominent citizens of New England.

Cheney presented Dartmouth College with a $50,000 scholarship, receiving about that time an Honorary Degree. In making this donation in 1880 Cheney requested that $40,000 be applied for a Professorship of Mathematics, the remainder to be divided between the Daniel Webster Professorship and the Presidential Fund. The letter he wrote contained these words:

> As a son of New Hampshire, I have for some time cherished the hope that I might be able to contribute in some way to the State which gave me birth. It occurs to me that I cannot do so in a more appropriate way than to donate a sum to Dartmouth College . . . with the request that upon consultation with the authorities of the institution you will have it applied in such manner as will in your judgment do the most good and produce the best results.

It is of special interest and little known that he gave a large sum to found an academy in a settlement in Washington territory which was named for the benefactor himself. His name was chosen owing to the fact that he was an original director of the Northern Pacific Railroad, which opened that territory.

Other gifts were made to other causes in which he was interested.

In 1854 an accident befell him at Canaan while on his way from Canada on the Northern New Hampshire Railroad. He went into the baggage car to talk over railroad matters with the operatives. While there the car was derailed and he lost his right arm by having it pinned in the wreckage. His many friends said that this unfortunate occurrence in no way affected his disposition or diminished his activity in business.

His great friend, Hon. Richard Olney, who was one of his executors, summed up his life in these words:

> Mr. Cheney was one of the self-made men of New England and possessed in large measure the qualities to which their success in life is to be attributed. From his youth up he was temperate, industrious, and persevering, and resolute in his purpose to better the conditions to which he had been born. He brought to its accomplishment great native shrewdness, a kindly, cheerful, and engaging disposition, a sense of honor, the lack of which often seriously impairs the efficiency of the strongest natures, and an intuitive and almost unfailing judgment of human character and motives. The reward of his career was not merely a large fortune accumulated wholly by honorable means, but the respect and regard of the entire community in which he lived.

An associate in business, the well-known Isaac T. Burr, said that he never knew a man who "possessed a greater sense of honor or sounder business judgment." It was this unusual sense of values and possibilities that enabled him to leave a substantial trust fund which is still in existence.

Mrs. Kaufmann, the only one of his children remaining, supplied a biographical sketch of her father which describes a tablet and boulder placed by his wife on the piece of land in Hillsborough, New Hampshire, where her husband was born in 1815; he died at his beautiful place at "Elm Bank" in Wellesley in the year 1895. This attractive estate became the property of another daughter, Mrs. W. H. Baltzell, where she and her husband lived for some years and where their visitors always enjoyed the well laid out grounds. Most of this property is now owned by the Stigmatine Fathers, an Italian order, as Dartmouth College did not care to assume it. Five elm trees were planted by Indian converts while at the nearby Nonantum Christian settlement.

The Cheney family is too well known to require much description of their ancestry, which begins on this side of the water as early as 1636 at Newbury when John Cheney settled there. An ancestor of Benjamin Cheney's wife was the Rev. Samuel Whiting of Lynn, who himself was a relative of the teacher at St. Botolph's Church in Boston, England. Cheney lived up to the motto of the English Cheneys: "Fato prudentia major" — "Wise energy is mightier than circumstances." His wife was Elizabeth Stickney Clapp of Dorchester, Massachusetts.

Cheney was named for the then Governor of New Hampshire, Benjamin Pierce, at the suggestion of the Governor, who also offered to send him to college, but the family decided that their son should go to a private school. He did, however, at the time of his being named receive a present of three sheep. The *New England Historic and Genealogical Register* goes on to explain that they had to be killed, unfortunately, because of a severe drought, but nevertheless "he entered life's tournament with the courage and sagacity of the Cheney family."

There are a number of clippings referring to the Cheney family history in the South Natick Library, copies of which were kindly sent us by Franklin Wyman of the State Mutual Life Assurance Company of Worcester.

It is a curious coincidence that Cheney's son, B. P. Cheney, Jr., met his death when he lost his way in the Arizona desert not far from the tracks of the Atchison Railroad of which he, too, was a Director.

SOME OLD CAMBRIDGE TAVERNS

THERE WERE several taverns in the old days in Cambridge which are worthy of mention. The first Blue Anchor Tavern goes back to 1652 and was frequented by the selectmen, several of the bills for "refreshments" being preserved, showing to what extent people indulged themselves in those days.

The original Blue Anchor Tavern was situated on the northeast corner of Brighton (now Boylston) and Mount Auburn Streets, opposite the Fox Club. It should be explained that as early as 1635 Boylston Street was a public highway known as Wood Street and later as Brighton Street, running down from what is now Harvard Square to the site of the "Great Bridge" erected about 1660. Mount Auburn Street was also a public highway in 1635 and was known as Spring Street. The so-called Market Place was situated on the westerly side of Boylston Street between Mount Auburn Street and Winthrop Street.

The first owner of this rather important inn was Andrew Belcher, who married the daughter of Nicholas Danforth, a Selectman of Cambridge and Representative to the General Court. Belcher and his wife Elizabeth removed with their family from Sudbury to Cambridge about 1645-6. In 1652 Andrew Belcher was "granted the liberty to sell beer and bread for entertainment of strangers and the good of the town" and later, in 1654, the County Court granted him a license "to keep a house of publique entertainment at Cambridge." His widow succeeded him and later his son Andrew became the owner. Other owners maintained the inn at the original location until 1737.

The second Blue Anchor Tavern, known also as the Anchor Tavern or as The Old Porter Tavern House, is described as being situated on the west side of Brighton Street, midway between Harvard Square and Mount Auburn Street. To this building the old sign was transferred in 1737, when Joseph Bean bought the house from Nathaniel Hancock. For nearly a century it was a famous gathering place, but we are informed by Clifford K. Shipton, Custodian of the Harvard University Archives, that of all the references and diaries in the library there are only unimportant mentions of this second tavern where probably many important events took place and where many students were wont to visit. Mr. Shipton reports to us that there are a number of references to these taverns in the College records, making mention of the fining of students for playing at cards and dice within their walls.

Paige's *History of Cambridge* mentioned that part of the old building, which housed the tavern, was still standing in 1877. The building probably was demolished about 1888 at the time Boylston Street was widened. The old records show that the southwesterly end of the tavern was about 100 feet northeasterly from Mount Auburn Street towards Harvard Square. There is a modern two-story brick building now in the middle of the block between Harvard Square and Mount Auburn Street occupied by Mandrake's Book Shop and by Corcoran's Department Store. The portion occupied by Corcoran's is on the site of this second Blue Anchor Tavern.

There was a Blue Anchor Tavern in Boston (often written "Blew") on land now occupied by the Globe newspaper building, also the site of the first official Post Office in our nation. The landlord, George Monk, was described as follows by John Dunton, the well-known London visitor here:

> A person so remarkable that, had I not been acquainted with him, it would be a hard matter to make any New England man believe I had been in Boston; for there was not one house in all the town more noted, or where a man might meet with better accommodation. Besides, he was a brisk and jolly man, whose conversation was coveted by all his guests as the life and spirit of the company.

Another tavern stood at Porter Square, a mile from Harvard Square, known as Porter's Tavern. Nearby there stood a gallows which was used occasionally to serve its grim function, and it is related that the following satirical lines were current at the time:

> Cambridge is a famous town,
> Both for wit and knowledge,
> Some they whip and some they hang,
> And some they send to college.

Mrs. Alice Morse Earle wrote that in 1755 many of the citizens of Cambridge and surrounding towns went from tavern to tavern to prepare themselves for some public punishment that was soon to take place. Mrs. Earle added: "On all these occasions the taverns flowed with good cheer and merry meetings, for people came for many miles to witness the interesting sight, and many were the reunions of friends."

In the writer's time, on the first spring-like day, a coterie of students used to celebrate the occasion by having a gin fizz and then sauntering out to Porter's Station and back to get the benefit of the warm fresh air.

Porter's Tavern is associated with the Hasty Pudding Club of Harvard University. Its first meetings were held in the rooms of members, as told by William McKim Garrison in an illustrated history of the Club. He quotes a sarcastic poem composed by a member, closing with the lines:

> When lo, by every eye and mouth rever'd,
> In Noyes' room the awful pot appear'd.

The savory dish (from which the Club got its name) was borne in by two of the members. On the birthday of George Washington, in the early years, the members used to march to Porter's Tavern, a custom which was continued for some time. The record speaks of a gala supper on one of these occasions, a piece of poetry reading:

> Thus was the mighty evening spent,
> And then to bed we soaring went.

At one time, owing to a fire, the Club had to move to a building on Jarvis Field, and in the conflagration pictures of many "ballet girls" were destroyed.

The late Robert S. Rantoul in a talk before the Essex Institute in Salem mentioned the students as they climbed on the stagecoaches to go home after their term had expired.

Has anybody forgotten the scene in College yard at Cambridge, when Peter Ray arrived at the end of the term, with his coach and six sorrels, to take home what might well be styled the "flower of Essex!" How he displayed, before admiring eyes, his mastery of curves and functions, by turning six-in-hand, at a cheerful trot, in the little corner between Holworthy and Stoughton, and how the Essex boys, cheered by their fellows, and eager for the long vacation, whirled out of college gate, and down the historic roads by Washington's Elm and Letchmere's Point, and Bunker Hill, to their welcome home! Handsome Peter, they called him — a favorite with children and ladies — for with him, on the introduction of the famous steel-spring coaches, they first knew what it was to ride comfortably outside, with an intelligent and entertaining driver, whose tongue kept pace with his team, and whose castles in the air often reached gigantic proportions before half the distance between Lynn and Salem was accomplished!

Porter's Tavern was a stopping place for sleighing parties which usually came out in large barges, stopping for "refreshments" of various kinds to help warm their constitutions for the return journey. It was situated at what is now the corner of Massachusetts Avenue and Porter Road and was still standing as late as 1903. Massachusetts Avenue was formerly known as North Avenue and this parcel was originally owned by the Porter family.

WOLFE TAVERN
Newburyport

Two CHIEF attractions connected with this well-known tavern are the unusual signboard and the stagecoach. The figure of General James Wolfe decorated several signs in pre-Colonial days. It was William Davenport, however, who hung out the original sign in 1762 when he made extensive alterations and additions to his home which he opened for the entertainment of travellers under the name of Wolfe Tavern. The building then stood on the corner of Threadneedle Alley and Fish Street (now Harris and State Streets) and was often spoken of as Davenport's Inn, also being known for a short time as the Merrimack Hotel.

The choice of the figure of General Wolfe as a design was prompted by the fact that Davenport, as a Captain, had served with the famous General on his historic expedition to capture Quebec. Davenport was on the Plains of Abraham in 1759 at the time of Wolfe's death and was also present when Quebec surrendered. The English General was a hero whose memory he wished to perpetuate, but little did he realize that his wish would continue to the present time.

Pauline A. Pinckney in her *American Figureheads and their Carvers* refers to Davenport as a "young carver of Newbury" and believes that he carved the Wolfe signboard. "His inn," she added, "became famous for its double bowls of rum punch and its egg and nipp toddies served with the gossip and religious and political discussions of the day." The Wolfe signboards on other inns were removed after the Declaration of Independence, but the landlord of this Newburyport tavern continued to keep his in use regardless of criticism.

Prince Stetson, one of the most noted of Newburyport landlords, took over the inn in 1807, and a copy of his announcement is reproduced here. Unfortunately the tavern was destroyed in the great Newburyport fire four years later.

There are various versions concerning the history of the Wolfe sign. It was doubtless the work of Moses Cole and when the fire occurred one account says that it was saved in some way and later was discovered in the dwelling of the noted Ben: Perley Poore of West Newbury. It was repainted by the same Moses Cole or else by someone whose name seems to be in doubt, and again found its place on the tavern wall. A Wolfe signboard is in use now, except in the winter months, but the date it was made cannot be ascertained.

A visit to this inn was made in 1868 by a writer for the *Newburyport Daily Herald* and the delightful report was sent to us by the Newburyport Public Library. The proprietor, Charles Little, had just expended many thousands of dollars to make the property "fully up to the height of fashion," and it was declared to be the finest hostelry between Boston and Portland. The reporter was told some of the stories of the eccentricities of the frequenters, one of which we will relate. A patron of the bar was handed a large bowl of punch and asked what he thought of it. Drinking down the whole of it at almost one gulp he remarked that all it needed was to be filled up again.

The article could not have been more complimentary, as will be seen by this enthusiastic statement:

> We might have said all that we have in one word, which is that the entire plan and all the arrangements of the house are simply perfect, and if the Merrimack House don't make Newburyport a place of summer resort, we shall almost think that Plum Island, Salisbury Beach, the Laurels, the Merrimack, and the score of places for bathing, boating, gunning, fishing, driving, botanizing, etc., in our immediate vicinity, were made in vain.

The same paper describes the tavern as appearing like a creation of Aladdin's lamp, but nevertheless believed that nothing could compare with the chickens of the days of the Davenports.

Many stages halted at the inn and in 1828 the Eastern Stage Line bought the property and had its headquarters there.

Prince Stetson & Co.

RESPECTFULLY INFORM THE PUBLIC,
That they have put in complete repair that well known
TAVERN, Formerly kept by Mr DAVENPORT,
SIGN OF
JAMES WOLFE ESQR.
State Street,
NEWBURYPORT.
Where those who favour them with their custom
shall experience every convenience and
attention which they can command

From "Stage Coach and Tavern Days" by Alice Morse Earle

A PRINCE STETSON HANDBILL OF WOLFE TAVERN, NEWBURYPORT,
MASSACHUSETTS, ENGRAVED BY WILLIAM HOOKER IN 1807.

Stetson was a well known landlord of this tavern from 1807 until the
building was destroyed by fire four years later. The James Wolfe signboard
can be seen in the foreground.

WOLFE TAVERN.

From "Ould Newbury" by John J. Currier

WOLFE TAVERN, NEWBURYPORT, MASSACHUSETTS

This successful company about that time owned 287 horses and many coaches. Much or all of this equipment was kept at the hostelry which was then known as the Old Stage Tavern, if not actually so named.

The second object of interest is the old stagecoach which is preserved in a back room adjoining the inn itself. The present owner and manager, Robert W. Weltshe, pointed out the chief parts connected with this huge vehicle, called by him a rugged, massive affair. One wonders how even six horses could drag it. One wonders also how anyone could stick to the forward seat or the back seats, over a rough road. Our guide told of an encounter between this coach, the city marshal and a parade that was passing through the town. The marshal yelled to driver Merrill to get out of the way and not to pass through the line of march. Merrill proved equal to the occasion and shouted back that he was carrying the United States mail which must get through. The parade was thereupon halted to permit the coach to proceed.

There are several other stagecoaches in Massachusetts that we know about, including those at the Wayside Inn and one owned by Miss Betty Dumaine of Groton, to be described in a later brochure.

First and last, many important persons have stopped at the Wolfe Tavern. Marquis de Chastellux, who had served under Rochambeau, came from France in 1782. He made the tavern his headquarters and wrote that:

It was two o'clock when we reached Merrimack ferry . . . After passing the ferry in little flat boats which held only five horses each, we went to Mr. Davenport's Inn where we found a good dinner ready. I had letters from Mr. Wentworth to Mr. John Tracy, the most considerable merchant in the place; but, before I had time to send them, he had heard of my arrival, and, as I was rising from table, entered the room, and very politely invited me to pass the evening with him.

That delightful writer and one of the leading citizens of Salem, Robert S. Rantoul, who was a veritable mine of informa-

From "History of Newburyport, Mass." by John J. Currier

OLD SIGNBOARD THAT ONCE HUNG ON THE WOLFE TAVERN IN
NEWBURYPORT, MASS.

The present sign was stored during the winter months and therefore a photograph could not be obtained.

tion, in a talk given in 1868 before the Essex Institute of Salem, entitled "Some Notes on Old Modes of Travel," quoted Hon. Allen W. Dodge, in which he mentions this inn:

And then too what a gathering at the old Wolfe Tavern in Newburyport, when the noon stage-coaches arrived from Boston. The sidewalk was often crowded with anxious boys, and men too, to catch a sight of distinguished passengers and the last fashions, and to hear the latest news. Why, it was as good as a daily paper, or a telegraphic dispatch — better indeed, for the living men, actors sometimes in the scenes described, were there to tell what had happened.

John Quincy Adams also spent a good deal of time in Newburyport and may have visited Wolfe Tavern on a number of occasions.

A visitor sees a large full length painting of an attractive woman, in the inn office. Upon inquiry it was explained that a Mr. Hannah who was the owner of a manufacturing plant in town admired Mrs. Charles Dana Gibson, the wife of the well-known artist, and had the picture painted. When his business came to a close, he presented the painting to the tavern. This incident was unknown to Mrs. Gibson until she was informed about it by the writer.

Sitting down to an excellent, simple meal one's attention is attracted to the four-panelled screen depicting in colors the Settlers of Newbury, Clam Houses, the Harbor and Whittier's birthplace in Haverhill. On the large menu appear the names of many people who have stayed there, including three Presidents of the United States. When the dishes are brought in it is seen that they are decorated with pictures of the tavern and the statue of William Lloyd Garrison which is situated nearby, close to another inn named *Garrison* connected by ownership with Wolfe Tavern. The bar of the latter is attractive, even excluding the various concoctions one may order.

The name *James Wolfe* not only appears on the signboard but on the mat at the entrance and at other places, as do the words "Where Your Ancestors Tarried."

STATE STREET TRUST COMPANY

MAIN OFFICE: COR. STATE & CONGRESS STREETS

*Ship models and old prints in an atmosphere
reminiscent of early Colonial counting houses.*

UNION TRUST OFFICE: 24 FEDERAL STREET

*Models, prints, etc., depicting the progress of avia-
tion from balloon and glider days to the present.*

STATE STREET TRUST COMPANY

MASSACHUSETTS AVE. OFFICE: COR. MASS. AVE. & BOYLSTON ST.

COPLEY SQUARE OFFICE: 587 BOYLSTON STREET

At each of our offices we have tried, by means of historical collections, to create an unusual and attractive atmosphere for those doing business with us.

STATE STREET TRUST COMPANY

BOSTON, MASSACHUSETTS

★

*MAIN OFFICE
Corner State and Congress Streets

★

UNION TRUST OFFICE
24 Federal Street

★

*MASSACHUSETTS AVENUE OFFICE
Massachusetts Avenue and Boylston Street

★

*COPLEY SQUARE OFFICE
587 Boylston Street

★

SALES FINANCE DEPARTMENT
581 Boylston Street

★

*Night Depository Service Available

★

Member Federal Reserve System
Member Federal Deposit Insurance Corporation